LIFE'S ANSWER SERIES

James Robison

ATTACK ON THE FAMILY

Tyndale House
Publishers, Inc.
Wheaton, Illinois

Seventh printing, March 1982

Library of Congress Catalog Card Number 80-51150
ISBN 0-8423-0092-9, paper
Copyright © 1980 by James Robison
Printed in the United States of America

CONTENTS

INTRODUCTION

"People are scared. They see relationships collapsing all around them, and they worry about whether theirs will last. But they don't know what to do about it."

This was a social scientist, Dr. Pepper Schwartz, commenting on the most disturbing phenomenon on the American scene—the collapse of marriage and the traditional family. People see what is happening, he was saying. They know that more than 55 percent of marriages now end in divorce and that the unmarried relationships touted by many of the intelligentsia have a far worse track record for permanence. They see the family deteriorating all about them. They sense the danger in the situation, but they "don't know what to do about it."

One reason they don't know is that they are being fed a confusing hodge-podge of advice from many different sources, some of it merely ill-conceived but much of it deliberately designed to destroy the institution of marriage and the traditional family structure.

You may say that you can understand why someone might offer bad advice on such an important matter out of ignorance, but why would anyone do so deliberately? The reason is that, for any one or a combination of reasons, they want to destroy marriage and the family as these institutions have been known in America.

Some desire this simply because they are libertine in their own lifestyles, and marriage and the home put a crimp in their ability to practice the immorality their hearts long for. God designed marriage and the home. They have rejected God, and they object to the very idea of anyone's prescribing a plan for their lives. Besides, the specifics of the plan annoy them. It prescribes one woman for one man, with the two cleaving to each other to achieve oneness in love. They want not one partner but as many as they choose to have. They don't want a permanent commitment with a responsibility to strive for oneness. They want to enjoy the thrills of exploiting another person's body as long as it pleases them, then discard that person and move on to another. That there could be pleasure and fulfillment in living to meet another person's needs is completely beyond their comprehension. They want the sensual pleasures of sex with no strings of responsibility attached.

God speaks of such people in the first chapter of Romans. He describes them as being given up to "uncleanness through the lusts of their own hearts, to dishonour their own bodies between themselves" (verse 24); as being given up to "vile (unnatural) affections" (verse 26), and to a "reprobate mind, to do those things which are not convenient" (verse 28). These "haters of God" (verse 30) want no part of God's plan for life, and they struggle to bar others from it, because they can't use and abuse those who are under God's protection.

Others seek to destroy marriage and the family because—in their prideful, atheistic high-minded-ness—they sincerely believe these institutions are outmoded and that the times call for new approaches to life. These are perhaps more dangerous to God's people than the other, because they often lead good moral lives and seem nobly motivated. They are the social activists, the intellectual movers and shakers who are constantly trying to solve society's problems. Unfortunately, since they have rejected God's solutions, the ones they offer seldom produce any lasting improvement in conditions. God refers to them in Romans 1 also, describing them as persons who, professing themselves to be wise, have become fools (verse 22). Seeing their plans fail and, in some cases, make matters worse never deters them from concocting new and more costly schemes. Not infrequently, they blame their failures on resistance from traditionalists and "religious fundamentalists." They equate both with ignorance and backwardness. They are bent on destroying marriage and the family because they see them as symbols of the past and obstructions to "progress."

There is a far more sinister threat to the home and family, however. This threat emanates from those who are out to destroy these institutions because they want to destroy America, or at least what has come to be known as "the American way of life." Why would they attack marriage and the home to destroy America? Simply because all that America has become—a strong, thriving nation, full of creativity, variety, and uniqueness—owes itself to the foundational influence of marriage and the family.

The family has been recognized for centuries as the basic social unit of civilization. In no culture, however, has the family played a more vital role in shaping the destiny of a nation than in America.

The home and family are the child's "school of life." In this intimate environment, children acquire their basic personalities. They learn the rules of conduct that make life livable for themselves and those with whom they come in contact. They acquire the wealth of knowledge they must have before they enter school, including the language that will be their basic means of communication for life.

The family is also the child's primary moral and spiritual instruction center. It is here that children internalize the moral values that guide their attitudes and behavior as they mature to adulthood. It is here that they receive their first and most lasting impressions concerning their own identity, the worth and dignity of others, and the fundamentals of relating properly to others. The home is also where the child develops the precepts on which he bases an understanding of God and spiritual truth. Thus, the home is the basis for the moral strength of the nation.

The American family has also proved itself the most effective economic institution the world has ever known. The family provides food, clothing, and shelter for the child, as well as a safe place for recreation and entertainment. The American family system supports more than 100 million persons, and does so in a way that builds their character and strengthens the social fabric of the country.

Historians of this and other countries have pointed to the home—the institutions of marriage and the family—as the backbone of America. As these institutions go, they have said, so will go the nation.

It stands to reason, then, that anyone who wanted to destroy the American way of life would single out marriage and the family as first-priority targets. This is especially true of those who scheme to replace the American system with some sort of collectivist state. Totalitarian governments thrive on conditions produced by disintegrating family life. They gain control of the populace by troubleshooting the problems that spring up like weeds in such an atmosphere—the women unable to support themselves; the abused and neglected children; the need for child-care facilities, early childhood education, values-orientation and health care, and such related problems as crime, drug-addiction, alcoholism, and mental illness. In the name of ministering to these problems, dictators and elitists create them and worsen them to provide an excuse for seizing power.

By weakening and destabilizing family life, these enemies of the home hope to make America easy prey for their efforts at thought control. A nation is hard to brainwash when most of its people are from stable families that have imparted to them a sense of security, independence, unique traditions, strong values, and a variety of wholesome attitudes on every facet of life. The collectivists would much prefer to work with the insecure, emotionally disturbed, poorly motivated products of a weak and unstable home environment. Unwholesome family life also creates economic dependency that the state is only too eager to exploit.

The collectivist goal, of course, is to make as many people as possible dependent on the state in as many ways as possible. When people are at the mercy of the state, they tend to be subservient to the state. The more ways in which they are dependent, the more ways in which they are subservient.

The literature of the collectivist slave systems is replete with methods for creating broadscale dependence on the state.

In *The Communist Manifesto*, for example, Karl Marx advocated:

—The abolition of property in land—which would undermine home ownership, one of the bases of family life.

—A heavy, progressive income tax—which would transfer economic power from the family to the state.

—Free (but compulsory) education for all children in public schools—which would enable the state to fill the minds of the young with its own ideas and values.

Some of the tactics and strategies used to attack the home include:

—Turning children against their parents by convincing them their elders are old-fashioned, ignorant, or out of touch with the realities of modern society.

—Encouraging sexual promiscuity (by indoctrination and by making contraceptives available to the young) as both healthy and fashionable—and ridiculing sexual purity as something for the wallflower and the prude.

—Promoting divorce as an acceptable and commonplace solution to marital problems, adultery as psychologically helpful to marriage, and fidelity as stuffy and oppressive.

—Promoting governmental policies whose effect is to force more wife-mothers out of the home and into the job market.

—Fostering schemes, such as the misleading Women's Lib movement, to create sexual hostility and antagonism within families and throughout society and to encourage men and women to abandon their traditional roles and responsibilities.

—Propagandizing the attitude that children are a nuisance, rather than a gift of God, and promoting widespread use of contraceptives to prevent pregnancy; also, promoting abortion as an acceptable form of birth control and clamoring for government child-care facilities to replace mothers in rearing the children that are allowed to be born.

—Striving, by subtle brainwashing and direct intimidation, to win acceptance for homosexuality and other forms of perversion as mere "alternate life-styles" or the marks of intelligence or social smartness.

—Eroding the religious base, sanctity, and moral significance of marriage, robbing the family of its sense of permanence and its spiritual effectiveness.

—Promoting the use of drugs, alcohol, and pornography, either overtly or covertly. Ostensibly, this is done to encourage expressions of personal and intellectual freedom, but actually to weaken the family.

These and other strategies, and the ways they are used in attacking the various elements of the family, will be discussed in greater detail. But even the little mentioned here may have alerted you to what the enemies of the home have been up to in your nation and in your community. Their tracks are to be seen everywhere you turn.

Consider the evidences of their effectiveness—the animosity between the sexes, the confusion of sex roles in the home and society, the gap in communication between parents and children, the sexual permissiveness, the disintegration of homes, the constant rise in drug and alcohol abuse, the epidemic of abortion, the increasing signs of emotional instability, irrational behavior, insecurity, mental illness.

Perhaps the most telling evidence of how well the anti-family strategies work is the growing role of government in family matters.

President Jimmy Carter announced in 1979 the establishment of an "Office for Families" within the Department of Health, Education, and Welfare. Noting that many families have been strained to the breaking point by social and economic forces "beyond their control," the President said the family had become an area of national life where a "partnership" of public and private interests is needed.

The President indirectly acknowledged that the state has a selfish interest in the well-being of the family. Families, he said, "are the foundation of a healthy and vibrant society." But he gave the impression that he genuinely envisioned the "Office for Families" as an agency to benefit the traditional family and to protect it from possibly harmful governmental policies and actions. He set up three White House Conferences on Families to be conducted in the summer of 1980 in Baltimore, Minneapolis, and Los Angeles. The purpose of these conferences, he said, would be to make a "long overdue assessment of how actions by government and major private institutions help, hurt, or neglect American families." The new office would help implement the recommendations of the conferences.

With humanist enemies of the family permeating government bureacracy, however, creating a government agency to help the family could be like putting the goats in charge of the cabbage patch. Enemies of the home like nothing better than masquerading as cavalry riding to the rescue of the beleaguered institution.

For example, no two more vehement enemies of the God-designed home may exist than Betty Friedan, founder of the National Organization for Women and acknowledged "mother of Women's Lib," and Muriel Fox, president of NOW's Legal Defense and Education Fund. Yet in 1979 they were talking like bold defenders of the family, as they were interviewed by UP reporter Patricia McCormick. This interview was printed in the Dallas *Morning News* of March 15, 1979. They were scoffing at the idea that the family is in "a hopeless state of collapse" and were committing their influence and resources to developing "innovative and practical solutions" to the family's problems.

The catch is that these two do not use the traditional definition for the word "family." They are talking about what they call "the evolved family." Here is the new definition: "Family is people who are living together with deep commitment and with mutual needs and sharing."

This redefining of the family seems quite calculated and deliberate. Ms. Fox and Ms. Friedan acknowledge "the old kind" of family still exists, but they say new (equally valid and acceptable) forms are emerging. And they emphasize that they would be promoting the new, finding "new ways to make the family, per se, livable, workable, lovable." They say the new forms are coming about "because men and women are living longer and don't want to be alone," the implied thought being that the "old kind" of family does not provide for the needs of all family members.

"I think some of these new families may even be stronger and richer in meaning (than the traditional family) as they emerge," Ms. Friedan said.

The Women's Legal Defense and Education Fund sponsored a meeting in the fall of 1979, a "National Assembly on the Future of the Family." It featured a braintrust of prominent figures from business, industry, and the professions. Explaining the purpose of the event, Ms. Fox said:

> Our assembly will be historic in that feminism
> is moving ahead to a new phase—designing
> solutions that will help families deal pro-

*ductively with the enormous opportunities—
and problems—resulting from the women's
movement as we free women, men, and children from old sex-stereotyped roles.*

With that statement, Ms. Fox summed up the
strategy employed by the feminist movement, not to
save the family but to wreck it. The strategy has
been to destroy the traditional or, more accurately,
the biblical roles of women, men, and children in the
home. Ms. Fox could speak with a certain sense of
gratification when she alluded to the problems
resulting from the demolition job the women's
movement has done on the American home.

Despite their initial insistence that the family is
surviving, Ms. Fox and Ms. Friedan noted that the
assembly would make certain assumptions, all of
which write off the biblically structured family as
already dead.

For instance, they said discussion leaders "will
accept rather than deny the fact that 93 percent of
American families today fit patterns other than the
traditional old pattern." This implies that only 7
percent of all families follow God's design for the
home. In saying the assembly would "accept" this
assertion as fact, the feminists were proclaiming
that their movement had already achieved its goal
of abolishing the traditional family.

Speakers would also, they said, "accept the inevi-
tability of continuing future change in the relationships and roles of men, women, and children within
families." Again the implication is that enemies of
the family are already victorious—in this case, in
their effort to destroy roles and relationships in the
home.

The tactic is to undermine their victims' will to resist by making it appear that the battle is over and that they have won. They give themselves away, however, by serving notice that they are still laboring tirelessly for the goals they claim already to have attained. Later in the same interview, Ms. Fox said:

> Through freeing men and women from old sex-stereotyped roles, feminism seeks to help all people achieve their full potential individually and in responsive relationships with others.
>
> Therefore, we are confident that feminism will ultimately lead to stronger, more varied, more nurturing and loving families.

This calls to mind the deceit used by Satan in pursuading Eve to eat of the forbidden fruit in the Garden. His strategy was to convince Eve that God was trying to cheat her, that by obeying God she was depriving herself of something very desirable and beneficial. Ms. Fox, expounding the feminist doctrine, asserts that freeing men, women, and children from their God-assigned roles enables them to "achieve their full potential." Once removed from God's plan and provision, she says in effect, they will find stronger, more loving families.

As though any human being apart from God could fulfill his or her potential! As though anyone apart from God could ever know the agape love which is the foundation of all successful human relationships!

The true impact of the humanist approach to helping people "achieve their full potential" is documented in some of today's objective social studies. Dr. Urie Bronfenbrenner, a Cornell psychologist, made the following assessment in an article in the

August 1974 issue of *Scientific American* titled "The Origins of Alienation":

Studies of human behavior have yielded few generalizations that are firmly grounded in research and broadly accepted by specialists, but there are two . . . that do meet these exacting criteria.

1. Over the past three decades literally thousands of investigations have been conducted to identify the developmental antecedents of behavior disorders and social pathology. The results point to an almost omnipresent overriding factor: *family disorganization.*

2. Much of the same research also shows that the forces of disorganization arise primarily not from within the family but from the circumstances in which the family finds itself and from the way of life that is imposed on it by those circumstances.

Specifically, when those circumstances and the way of life they generate undermine relationships of trust and emotional security between family members, when they make it difficult for parents to care for, educate, and enjoy their children, when there is no support or recognition from the outside world for one's role as a parent and when time spent with one's family means frustration of career, personal fulfillment, and peace of mind, then development of the child is adversely affected. The first symptoms are emotional and motivational: disaffection, indifference, irresponsibility, and inability to follow through in activities requiring application and persistence. In less favorable *family circumstances the reaction takes the form of antisocial acts injurious to the child and society. Finally, for children who come from environments in which the capacity of the family to function has been most severely traumatized by such destructive forces as poverty, ill health, and discrimination, the consequences for the child are seen not only in the spheres of emotional and social maladjustment but also in the impairment of the most distinctive of human capacities: the ability to think, to deal with concepts and numbers at even the most elementary level.*

Anyone who pays attention to conditions in society knows that all of these symptoms of family disorganization exist—and in far more pronounced form than they did in 1974, when Dr. Bronfenbrenner wrote his article.

Some of the "forces of disorganization" may be labeled the predictable results of rampant materialism in an industrialized society. But the enemies of the home have busied themselves aggravating these "natural" circumstances that tug at the foundations of the family, as well as creating as many new ones as they can.

In the pages that follow, the handiwork of those who have set out to destroy the home and the American way of life will be revealed in stark detail. The presentation will by no means be a complete documentation of their skulduggery. The evidence is simply too voluminous to be aired exhaustively in any one book. What is presented, however, may be shocking to some who haven't realized how late the hour is for the traditional family. It may be depressing at times to those who know the beauty of God's perfect plan for marriage and the home.

But I urge readers to remember two things. First, the enemies of the home are lying when they claim to have already won the war. There are millions of decent people, non-Christians as well as Christians, who are upholding the traditional roles and structures of the family throughout America. If these people unite and commit themselves to battle, the family can still be saved. Second, I would ask all Christians to remember the words of our Lord in John 16:33: "In the world ye shall have tribulation: but be of good cheer; I have overcome the world."

ONE

TARGET: THE HUSBAND-FATHER

The story of El Cid, the legendary Spanish hero of the eleventh century, holds an important moral lesson for modern America. The enemies of El Cid's cause knew well the secret of the success of his armies—their leader. Dispose of El Cid, they reasoned, and his forces would collapse like the proverbial sand castle. In the next encounter, one detachment of enemy forces was assigned to attack the great leader himself. Ignoring the rest of the battle, these special troops were to fight their way to El Cid and shower him with spears and arrows until they had wounded or killed him. They accomplished their mission. The brilliant and inspired leader rode back to his castle mortally wounded. Before dawn, he died.

As the enemy had predicted, when El Cid's soldiers took the field without him the next morning, they were mere shadows of the indomitable fighting force they had been the day before. Seeing the carnage developing on the battlefield, El Cid's commanders dressed his body in his armor, propped it on a horse and trotted the horse through the castle gates. Thinking their leader still alive and able to guide them, El Cid's men fought with superhuman ferocity and defeated the enemy.

Today, the enemies of the American home know that its strength depends primarily on leadership of the husband-father. Like the enemies of El Cid, they are aiming the brunt of their attack against the leader. If they can destroy the husband-father—if they can prevent him from fulfilling his God-assigned mission in the family—they know the home will quickly disintegrate. Knowing this enemy strategy, Christians should be doing everything within their power to uphold the husband-father, to support him and help insure that he succeeds in all his roles as head of the family.

That task won't be easy, because the attacks are both subtle and fierce, and the enemy already has occupied more strategic ground than most Christians seem to realize. In almost every role given him, the husband-father faces withering fire from those seeking to destroy his effectiveness. Let's take the husband-father's roles one at a time and examine the assaults mounted against each.

PROVIDER

Through the ages, the husband-father has been regarded as the one primarily responsible for providing the material needs of the family. Today, men are under vicious attack in this role.

Some of the ammunition used in this attack has been supplied by the world system as manifested in American culture. Material success, the accumulation of wealth, receives great emphasis in our society. At the same time, an individual's progress in achieving this type of success has become highly conspicuous. It can be measured by the make and model of car he drives, the size and location of his house, the clothing he and his family wear, and the schools his children attend. Men are under constant pressure to be "good providers" in this visible, material sense.

In the marketplace where he goes to prove himself as a provider, the husband-father experiences still more pressure. He is likely to work at a job that requires close supervision. His every move may be subject to critical examination. If he makes a mistake or fails in the slightest to perform up to expectations, he may be reprimanded or belittled. Such job situations can keep a man constantly questioning his own worth, his prowess as a provider, and his ability to hold up under the pressures closing in on him. Always hanging over him, of course, is the possibility of that crowning blow—loss of job.

If the husband-father had only these built-in pressures of the world system to cope with, he would have his hands full. But the enemies of the home have made his task immeasurably greater. They have found ways to magnify the pressures he faces, to distort them and aim them at him from many different and unexpected directions.

HUSBAND

The impact of all of these pressures, cultural and contrived, lands hardest on the man's role as husband. The husband, according to God's plan, is "head of the wife" and spiritual leader of the home (Ephesians 5:23 25). In this role, he is responsible not only for managing the home's financial affairs but also for meeting the physical, psychological, and spiritual needs of his wife. His enemies are erecting every conceivable obstacle to prevent him from fulfilling this vital role.

First, they are fostering confusion and ambiguity concerning the nature of his role. Not many years ago, a man had no problem defining his responsibilities. He knew what was expected of him. If he listens to the voices of the world—and it's almost impossible to avoid them—he may not now be able to define what a man is, much less what one is supposed to do.

Once it was clear that the man worked outside the home to earn the living while the woman took care of the meals, house, clothes, and kids. Now nearly half of all married women work outside the home. As the woman has come to share the provider role, the man has been called on to share her duties as mother and housewife. Dedicated husbands have always helped their wives with the chores, and that is as it should be. But in the past men did so with a clear understanding of the difference between the roles of the husband and the wife. Such pitching in to help in time of need and the current wave of confusion over roles and responsibilities are two entirely different things. Again, conditions built into modern culture form the basis for the confusion. But the enemies of the home are deliberately intensifying the ambiguity to weaken the leadership of the husband and drive a wedge of friction and conflict between him and his wife.

Much of this assault against the role of the husband comes from the feminist movement. Some feminist spokespersons claim, in encouraging women to leave their roles and pursue careers outside the home, that men will find career women more interesting. This will actually strengthen their marriage relationships, they say. While this may be so in some cases, it is by no means universally true. In fact, the burden of evidence indicates that the confusion in roles is striking at the man-woman relationship itself, at sex orientation, the very basis of that relationship. Most developments suggest that as women become more like men in the way they dress and act and the jobs they do, they are less liked by men.

A special aired some time ago by NBC-TV contained several indications that some of those pushing the so-called "sexual revolution" know what its true impact will be on relations between men and women. Titled "Of Women and Men," it featured Barbara Walters and Tom Snyder. It predicted a society in which marriages would not be permanent commitments but "serial" and "contractual" arrangements. These relationships would be formed not on a basis of love or physical oneness but on a basis of "equality." At one point in the discussion, Ms. Walters said:

> Well, it may be that women are playing the parts of husbands. They may be earning more of the income. They may be on the executive level. . . . It seems there's going to be some fear on the part of the men. It will mean that there will be further competition in the economic market, but on the other hand, we will be tapping people (women) we never have used before.

In a world in which sex roles are confused, men are ceasing to look on women as persons deserving special honor and respect, as potential life mates and mothers. They are regarding them as competitors who, by government decree, enjoy undeserved advantages in the contest for jobs and status. They see them as creatures to be despised and even feared. Men not led by the Spirit of God have always mistreated women. But, ironically, the feminist movement, with tactics calculated to liberate women from this mistreatment, is assuring that men will more than ever before consider women as objects for exploitation or, as Barbara Walters let slip, resources to be "used."

Further contributing to this attitude toward women are the Playboy philosophy, the upsurge of hard-core pornography, and the sexual permissiveness promoted by almost every facet of modern society. All of these forces tend to confuse men concerning what women are and how they are to relate to women.

By attacking the basic sexual orientation of the man, the enemies of the home are striking at something very basic to the man's ability to fulfill his functions as a husband. In his book *The New Chastity and Other Arguments Against Women's Liberation*, antifeminist author Midge Decter emphasizes this point:

> For a man, sex is an attainment like the other attainments of his life; it is indeed often felt by him to be paradigmatic of them: each incidence of potency in bed providing some intestinal reassurance of his adequacy to deal with the world outside it.

Thus, some social scientists, at least, are aware that the sexual identity of the male is closely related to his ability to perform, not just as a mate to his wife, but as a man in the world. It stands to reason that the enemies of the home are also cognizant of this fact. Would Christians be wandering too far afield if they speculated that these enemies know perfectly well that in their assault on man's sexual identity they are undermining the very foundations of his role as husband and head of the home?

In their effort to turn the husband's sexuality into a weapon to destroy marriages, enemies of the home get plenty of help from a perverse society and greedy entrepreneurs who are interested in nothing but the fast buck. Writer George Gilder, in his book *Sexual Suicide,* (published in 1973 by Quadrangle Publishers) reveals why men are so vulnerable to this enemy attack. He says:

*Most young men are subject to nearly unremit-
ting sexual drives, involving their very identities
as males. Unless they have an enduring relationship with a woman—a relationship that affords
them sexual confidence—men will accept almost any convenient sexual offer. . . . The
existence of a semi-illegal, multi-billion dollar
pornography market, almost entirely male ori-
ented, bespeaks the difference in sexual character between men and women.*

God created man a sexual being—"male and female
created he them" (Genesis 1:27). The husband's sexual drives are God-given. But God meant for all of
man's needs and appetites to be submitted to his
control (Romans 6:13), and he provided for man's
sexual drives to be fulfilled by his wife in the oneness
of the marriage relationship (Genesis 2:24).

Down through the ages, Satan has tempted men to
deviate from God's plan in fulfilling their sexual
drives. In a society such as ours, these temptations
become overwhelming. The mass communications
media are saturated with sex. Sexual permissiveness
and deviations from biblical sexual behavior are
encouraged even in the schools and colleges, so much
so that young women are made to feel ashamed and
unworthy if they maintain their virginity. As a result,
some studies show that more than half of our teenage
girls have had premarital sex by the time they are
eighteen.

In the midst of this permissive atmosphere, the
pornographer's sinister trade flourishes. Preying on
the strong sex drives of boys and men, the porno-
graphic picture, book, or movie teases men to seek
sexual pleasures forbidden by God because of their

destructiveness to the personality, the marriage union, and the stability of society.

I offer no excuses for the husband who gives in to these temptations, sacrificing his marriage and his family on Satan's altar of sexual indulgence. But of this I am thoroughly convinced: Apart from a spiritual rebirth and a life committed to the control of the indwelling Holy Spirit, no man is likely to withstand for very long the continuous assault being made against his sexual morality by the devil and his antifamily allies.

The success of this particular assault on the home is seen on every hand—in the increase in extramarital "affairs" by men, in the failure of men to find fulfillment in the marriage union that God designed for them, in the number of men turning to homosexuality and bizarre sex behavior in search of new "thrills."

The enemies of the home know what they are doing in attacking through the husband's sexuality, and they are doing a workmanlike job of it. Churches and individual Christians—particularly Christian wives—should be praying and doing everything God empowers them to do to support men in their husband role and protect them against the vicious tactics of the enemy.

FATHER

In his role as a father, the man plays a significant part in the personality development of the children. It was once thought that the mother was the more important parent in the area of child-rearing. Now, however, social scientists are discovering what Bible-believing Christians have known all along—that the father is in a position to have the greater influence in shaping the personality of the child.

Sociologists and psychologists say the father is the one who contributes most to the development of basic elements of personality. These include:

Confidence—assurance of worthiness, of ability to perform as expected.

Independence—ability to make decisions, and to make the type that in most instances prove wise and constructive.

Achievement orientation—an inclination to establish reasonable goals, adopt worthy projects, and put forth the effort needed to accomplish them.

Self-discipline—diligence in behavior that promotes the well-being of the child and of other persons and inhibits harmful or undesirable behavior.

Morality—the acquiring of a sense of values and a lifestyle that conforms to the values adopted.

Sex-typing—the development of wholesome attraction for the opposite sex.

The social scientists have also discovered that the father contributes to these personality traits through countless actions and attitudes, whether or not he is aware of what he is doing. For example, just by leaving home and returning at the same times, almost every day, a father lays important groundwork for the development of self-discipline in the child. From this the child learns the importance of time and the concept of scheduling or budgeting time. By the way the father plays with the child and by the things he does with him, he makes tremendous contributions to all the basic personality elements.

The crucial ingredient in the father's contribution is what I call "the difference factor." In his first weeks and months in the world, a child is most exposed to the mother. The father represents a person who is "different." He doesn't do the same things with the child that the mother does. He doesn't look or act like the mother. His activities with the child are more likely to be exhilarating and exciting and somewhat rougher than the mostly care-taking activities of the mother. The father's activities also are likely to be more wide ranging, exposing the child to a greater variety of experiences. Thus, from the father the child begins to acquire an ability to cope with unfamiliar experiences, people, and places.

All that the child experiences with this "different" person is highly stimulating, both emotionally and intellectually. For this reason, the father is the most important figure in the child's life from the standpoint of "observational learning." In other words, a child becomes much of what he or she will grow up to be simply by watching Dad.

That's a little frightening, isn't it? It's even more disturbing in light of the number of children who are growing up in fatherless homes in America today, with no "Dad model" to watch.

The enemies of the home know the importance of the father in the personality development of children, and they have launched an unrelenting effort either to drive the father out of the home or to undermine his effectiveness in the child-rearing role.

The enemies have working for them the cultural forces I mentioned at the beginning of the chapter. The pressures heaped on the father in his role as provider keep many men on their jobs too long each day. To meet high living costs—and the costs of high living—an increasing number of fathers hold two or more jobs. In our highly mobile industrialized society, many men hold traveling jobs that take them out of town for several days at a time or "shift" jobs that keep them away from home in the evenings and at night, sometimes even on weekends.

You can understand the roadblocks these cultural forces toss in the path of a man trying to fulfill his role as a father. The activities by which a father contributes to the development of his children's personalities have one common requirement—time. To fulfill his childrearing role, a father must spend time with his children, even if only a few minutes every day. The pressures attacking the father through his provider role restrict the amount and quality of time a father can spend with his children.

Another cultural condition that militates against the father is the mobility of young people. Because of their access to cars, many owning their own, teenagers often travel away from the home for entertainment, recreation, and other activities. Not only are they beyond the view of their parents, but they are often without any adult supervision. This make it doubly difficult for the father to discipline the children or to engage in other character-forming activities with them.

Enemies of the home are not content to let these cultural forces take their toll on the effectiveness of the father. They are busily at work creating more problems for him.

One of their most effective strategies has been to prevent fathers from fulfilling their responsibilities as head disciplinarian in the home. The offensive against the father in this regard has been moving forward on several fronts for a number of years.

Psychologists began decades ago to promote a permissive approach to child-rearing. They started with mild exhortations against paddling and progressed to advocating that children should be allowed to do virtually as they please without challenge or reprimand from their parents. Now almost all the information and advice society offers parents on child-rearing is of highly permissive variety. As a result, any father who adheres to biblical methods of disciplining his children faces serious problems. Because his values differ from those of society, he may have guilt feelings. If his neighbors find out about him, he may be criticized and ostracized. His children, when they realize they are being subjected to a stricter and more physical brand of correction than their friends, may misunderstand their father's motives and rebel.

Foes of the home are ever alert for opportunities to encourage rebellion against the father. Their strategies in this regard will be discussed in more detail later, in the chapter on the attack against children. At this point I will only touch on the sources and general nature of the most telling attacks being directed at the father through his children.

One source of attack is the mass media: newspapers, magazines, movies, and television—especially the latter. In recent years, stories, articles, and comments appearing in these media have increasingly encouraged children to make decisions without the advice and direction of their parents. Many urge outright defiance of parental guidance. "You've got to be you" is the predominant theme.

Not only are children encouraged to declare independence from their parents, but they are also given the impression that Dad would be too dumb to guide them even if they were willing to listen to him. The idea that "father knows best" is passe'in the media. It has been replaced by "father knows less."

Fathers may have been held in a bit too high esteem in the past. Children need to realize that Dad isn't someone who can do no wrong. But the current demotion of the father to the level of a buddy at best, and a not very bright one at that, is a dangerous step in the wrong direction. It is eroding the American young person's respect for authority not only in the home but in society.

Another source of attack against the father's role in child-rearing is the public schools. I am not opposed to public education, and I deeply appreciate the many fine teachers who toil at marginal salaries to prepare our children to enter society as strong, productive citizens. But many schools, textbooks, and teachers today exert an influence that makes it all but impossible for a father to rear his children by biblical methods.

First, the overall trend is to teach children that they are to develop their own values. They are not to accept the values of their parents or other authority figures, such as the church. Religious instruction is banned from the schools by the doctrine of church-state separation as interpreted by the U. S. Supreme Court. As a result, children tend to acquire a Godless perspective of life in many schools. Without God as the ultimate authority, there are no absolute values. Thus, a child's values are as valid as anyone else's— including his father's.

Corporal correction, paddling, is prohibited in most schools. Not only that, it is condemned in most school literature and classroom instruction.

Exposed to these ideas day after day, children with fathers who have strong, Bible-based convictions and who discipline according to biblical methods are programmed for rebellion. Their school experience influences them to look on their fathers as old-fashioned if not downright cruel. Then we wonder why so many fathers seem to lose control of their kids and why so many kids resent and resist any attempt by anyone to exert authority over them!

A casualty report from the attack against the home through the husband-father would include many items hard to enumerate and measure—unhappy marriages, miserable families, including children who grow up with an improper sex orientation, little self-confidence and self-discipline, no initiative or perseverance, impaired learning ability, and ill-defined or grossly distorted moral values.

But other casualties can be counted, and the toll is a grim one: Tens of thousands of deserting fathers and runaway children; a divorce rate of 55 percent—tops in the industrialized world; one-parent homes (most headed by mothers) increasing at a rate of three million per decade.

The measurable impact on husband-fathers themselves is worth noting. They die an average of seven years younger than wife-mothers, are far more likely to commit suicide, constitute a majority of the alcoholics and drug addicts, and commit five-sixths of the serious crimes.

America's husband-fathers are fighting a losing battle. They need all the reinforcements the church and the individual Christian can rush to their defense.

TWO

TARGET: THE WIFE-MOTHER

"The hand that rocks the cradle is the hand that rules the world," wrote William Ross Wallace over a century ago. And while that may be an exaggeration of the woman's influence on the course of human events, it makes the important point that God has given the wife-mother an indispensable role in shaping the home and society. The Lord seems to have endowed women with special traits that enable them to fulfill their role in the face of greatest adversities. When women are denied the opportunity to make their unique contribution, society suffers bitter consequences. One of our Founding Fathers, John Adams, recognized this when he said:

> From all that I had read of history and government, of human life and manners, I had drawn this conclusion, that the manners of women were the most infallible barometer, to ascertain the degree of morality and virtue in a nation. . . . The Jews, the Greeks, the Romans, the Swiss, the Dutch, all lost their public spirit, their republican principles and habits, and their republican forms of government, when they lost the modesty and domestic virtues of their women.

The enemies of the home are fully aware of the importance of woman to the permanence of marriage, the stability of the family, and the rearing of children. That explains why their attack on women, in all their various roles, is as determined as their assault on men—and in some ways even more direct and daring.

The roles of the woman in the home, like those of the man, are inseparably intertwined, overlapping, and complementary. For the sake of this discussion, I am classifying her responsibilities under three headings—housewife, mate, and mother—and I will show some ways in which the enemy is attacking in each category.

When the attack on the home through the woman is mentioned, the first "enemy" that pops into the minds of most Bible-believing Christians is "Women's Lib," the feminist movement. There are good reasons for such a reaction, and I will deal at length with the fierce onslaught against the home from that quarter.

However, I must first mention the ammunition that other enemies of the home have provided for the Libbers.

In our culture, women have historically been given an exalted and protected position. That is because our culture developed under the strong influence of New Testament Christianity. Our laws reflect the general attitude of respect displayed toward women in our society. These include laws exempting women from military combat, protecting them from certain types of working conditions, providing legal grounds for their support when widowed or divorced, and making fathers responsible for the support of their children. All such laws can be traced to Christian principles and the elevated position given women by Jesus, the Apostles, and the early church.

Unfortunately, the biblical imperatives for treating women with honor and respect have been no more immune to violation than any other instructions in the Word of God. Some men have always used their God-ordained role as head of the home as an excuse to dominate and demean their wives psychologically and physically. Some have always regarded women as sex objects existing to satisfy their lusts for physical pleasure, rather than as the precious life-mates God created them to be. Some have always treated them like domestic servants good for nothing but to do the cooking, mopping, and ironing and to keep the children quiet when the man is at home. Some have always dedicated themselves to defiling and corrupting women, instead of loving them and purifying them as Christ does the church (Ephesians 5:25, 26). In the marketplace, many employers have exploited women, paying women less than men for the same work and responsibility and denying them benefits and opportunities for advancement offered men of comparable performance and potential.

To deny that women have been mistreated would be as foolish as to claim there is no sin in the world—no lust, no greed, no hatred, no meanness, no violence. However, though the mistreatment of women stems not from Christian concepts but from defiance or distortion of those concepts, it has provided the bitterness that enemies of the home are now using to recruit women to their cause. To the extent that the feminists' homewrecking efforts and other activities are causing problems for corrupt, exploiting men and institutions, they can be regarded as divine judgment for long-unpunished transgressions. And to the extent that these transgressions are continuing, they can themselves be deemed attacks on the home and family.

The architects of the feminist movement have shown unbelievable skill and imagination in hammering the sins of the exploiters and lechers into spears for attacking the home. My frustration in preparing this book has not been in finding evidence of the attack but in sifting through the mounds of proof and deciding which bits to include in my discussion. As you read, I think you will be forced to agree that the evidence reveals that women, in each of their roles, are the target of a dangerous enemy thrust against the home.

HOUSEWIFE

Many feminist leaders are like that unreliable white man the Indians used to complain about. They speak with forked tongue. On the one hand, they protest that they are being misrepresented when people accuse them of demeaning the role of housewife-mother. They insist they are only saying that a woman should be allowed to choose a career outside the home without being stigmatized. On the other hand, they quite clearly belittle the role of housewife-mother at almost every opportunity, and their own writings and utterances reveal that one of their primary goals is to abolish the housewife role in society.

In the role of housewife, the woman's responsibility is to create a cheerful and wholesome atmosphere in which she and her husband can achieve oneness in their marriage relationship and in which children can grow and mature physically, psychologically, and spiritually.

The role includes unlimited opportunities for creativity. The preparation of meals, provision of clothing, and decoration and arrangement of the home can be—and should be—challenging creative opportunities. Even the routine chores—cleaning, washing, ironing, and doing the dishes—are services that women with hearts of love have always done cheerfully for their husbands and children. Loving husbands and children have shared the burden of the less pleasant and more strenuous chores. In homes where each family member follows God's plan for his life, the housewife finds fulfillment of a degree that society offers few other women.

With their skillful propaganda, however, the Women's Liberationists have managed to make the housewife's role seem one of uninterrupted drudgery. They have glamorized careers in the marketplace to such an extent that women who remain in the home, when asked what they do, almost automatically say, "I'm *just* a housewife." They have won wide acceptance for the idea that only a dummy would stay in the house all day and "slave" for a husband and a bunch of kids.

The tone for feminist propaganda was set by Betty Friedan, credited with launching the feminist movement, in her book, *The Feminine Mystique* (published in 1963 by Norton Publishers). By "feminine mystique" Ms. Friedan means the traditional image women have held in our culture, which is patterned after the biblical image. She assails this "mystique" as an instrument of oppression that has made "housewife-mothers, who never had a chance to be anything else, the model for all women." She goes on to say:

> It (the "feminine mystique") presupposes that history has reached a final and glorious end in the here and now, as far as women are concerned. Beneath the sophisticated trappings, it simply makes certain concrete, finite, domestic aspects of feminine existence as it was lived by women whose lives were confined, by necessity, to cooking, cleaning, washing, bearing children — into a religion, a pattern by which all women must now live or deny their femininity.

Ms. Friedan cleverly concedes that many housewife-mothers seem blissfully happy in their roles. She even paints a beautiful picture of one who seems to have built a very fulfilling life, finding enjoyment in her home and family as she efficiently performs her household chores. Then, with one poisonous stroke of the pen, she defaces this heartwarming portrait.

"Staring uneasily at this image," she says, "I wonder if a few problems are not somehow better than this smiling empty passivity. If they are happy, these young women who live the feminine mystique, then is this the end of the road?"

With such subtle, crafty insinuations, Ms. Friedan and other feminist propagandists have stirred doubt and discontent in the hearts of millions of women who enjoyed happy, fulfilled lives as housewives and mothers. They have succeeded in persuading many women to feel ashamed and guilty if they are happy and contented in the role of housewife. This cynical feminist assault on what they call "smiling, empty passivity" is an attack on God's blueprint for the ideal wife and mother, and the tactics they use are familiar. Ask a rhetorical question—like, "Doesn't your being happy just show that you're a bit simple, a bit empty-headed?" Follow it by another: "Aren't you missing something just because you don't have the nerve to stick your head outside the home and run the risk of a few problems?"

They couldn't have done their work better if they had gone to school in the Garden of Eden and observed as the serpent demonstrated on Eve, slyly asking, "Yea, hath God said . . . ?"

Magazines, especially a number of new ones aimed at "liberated" women, are full of articles denigrating housewives and glorifying careers in the marketplace. Typically, they urge housewives to get a job, then exhort them to adopt the animalistic behavior of lecherous men. The language is anything but subtle in some articles, such as this one from *New Woman* magazine in 1976, in which these paragraphs appeared:

> *Women must make their own lives; we must not expect a man to make our life for us. Work is the constant, not another person. The "housewife" appears to have what the rest of us claim is obsolete—security in another person.*
>
> *The need to achieve isn't new to women: only the accessible routes to achievement are new. A country's worth of opportunity has just opened to women—the jobs are there, the responsibility, possibility, authority, power, engagement, money, excitement.*

No discussion of the attack on the home through the woman as housewife would be complete without a word about the Equal Rights Amendment, the feminist cause célèbre.

Feminist propagandists have promoted the constitutional amendment as simply an instrument to assure women of equality in the marketplace—equal pay for equal work, etc.—and equal treatment under the law. In its innocuous wording, the ERA sounds like it would be only that: "Equality of rights under the law shall not be denied or abridged by the United States or by any state on account of sex."

Many who have studied the ERA and its implications for society see in its innocent wording a threat of wholesale social and legal disruption. For example, in his testimony before a congressional committee during the ERA debate in 1970, Harvard Professor Paul Freund said:

Not every legal differentiation between boys and girls, men and women, husbands and wives, is of an obnoxious character, and . . . to compress all these relationships into one tight little formula is to invite confusion, anomaly, and dismay.

Dr. Jonathan H. Pincus, professor of neurology at the Yale Medical School, put it even more bluntly in an article in the *New York Times* of October 24, 1971.

If family stability plays an important role in the well-being of our nation, it is hard to envision the Equal Rights Amendment . . . as a constructive act. One must agree with women's liberation groups that the liberating effect of Equal Rights will apply to men as well as to women. What they are both being liberated from is nothing less than the restrictions of traditional roles in a family structure.

Is this really the goal of the feminist in pushing for the ERA? Are they actually out to scramble the traditional roles and blur or obliterate the differences between men and women in the social structure?

A clue may be found in the scenario surrounding a series of proposed amendments to the Equal Rights Amendment. Offered by Sen. Sam Ervin of North Carolina, the amendments would not have affected the equal rights aspect of the measure. They would merely have preserved laws providing special consideration and protection for women. Specifically they would have:

—Exempted women from combat duty.
—Exempted them from the military draft.
—Preserved laws protecting working women in the marketplace.

—Preserved traditional legal protection for wives, mothers, and widows.

—Kept fathers responsible for support of their children.

—Maintained laws securing privacy to men or women, boys or girls on the basis of sex.

—Substituted for the original ERA this wording: "Neither the United States nor any State shall make any legal distinction between the rights and responsibilities of male and female persons unless such distinction is based on physiological or functional differences between them."

You might understand how militant feminists could object to the change in basic wording of the ERA. What is interesting, however, is that they fought the other proposed amendments tooth and toenail.

Clearly, they saw these changes as barriers to their real goal, which is a complete sex-role revolution and total destruction of the role of housewife.

A 1972 incident proves beyond the shadow of a doubt that this is the true crux of the matter. The Civil Rights Office of the Health, Education, and Welfare Department ruled that, under Title IX of the Education Amendments enacted that year, such public school events as father-daughter banquets and mother-daughter teas constituted illegal sex discrimination. President Gerald Ford ordered the ruling suspended immediately. In the furor stirred by the incident, much of the press denounced the ruling and yet dismissed it as merely the senseless act of some dingbat bureaucrat.

Feminists, however, were furious with the President for interfering with the ruling, which they regarded as an entirely logical enforcement of the law as they understood its purpose. Those who doubt that the feminists are bent on destruction of existing sex roles need only listen to the remarks of one of their leading proponents, syndicated columnist Jane O'Reilly, following the Title IX debacle. She wrote in the *Washington Star:*

> No one whom I have read or heard has stopped to ask why HEW made its decision. Everyone has assumed that one-parent exclusive school events are good things, and HEW wrong and stupid. The assumption indicates how lightly people skim over the implications of equality for women ... Title IX of the Civil Rights Act of 1972 is designed to interfere with those traditional systems and structures of discrimination.

Anti-feminist Phyllis Schlafly wrote of the episode:

> This flap clearly shows what is wrong with a simple sounding law that flatly bars all "sex discrimination." Rational people don't see anything wrong about discrimination against men by having a Mother-Daughter Breakfast, etc.
>
> This proves the radical, extreme goal for a gender-free society. You will be forbidden by law to separate men and women or treat them differently any time, for any purpose, no matter how worthy, or how much desired by the majority. This is the goal of ... the Women's Lib movement, and ... they intend to pursue this goal by federal enforcement.

Mrs. Schlafly noted that in this case the President had been able to rescind the federal agency's ruling and that if the courts held against the President, Congress could remedy the problem by amending the 1972 act under which the ruling was issued. Then she put her finger on the real danger inherent in the Equal Rights Amendment:

> . . . If ERA is in the Constitution, no phone call by the President, and no amendment by Congress, can do anything to prevent the absolute nonsense that will be required. Why? Because the U.S. Constitution is "the supreme law of the land," and it supersedes any other law or ruling.

Even without the ERA, the feminist movement, working with the pressures generated by a materialistic, pleasure-oriented culture, has made remarkable progress in attacking the home through the housewife.

Statistics available at this writing show that 58 percent of the nation's mothers hold jobs outside the home. Working women, says Professor Eli Ginzberg, chairman of the National Commission for Manpower Policy, is "the single most outstanding phenomenon of this century." (From his book *Lifestyle of Educated Women*, published in 1966 by Columbia University Press.) They make up 41 percent of the total U. S. work force. That means 41 million working women, and the number increases daily. Of every 100 new jobs created by the economy, 60 are being filled by women. Three in five families that include a husband and wife now have two or more wage earners.

Not only are women working in unprecedented numbers, but they are invading traditionally masculine fields. There are women police officers—not dispatchers or paper handlers but patrolmen on the beat. There are women firefighters, truck drivers, and mechanics. And the President has proposed the drafting of women for military duty.

The President's move was preceded by a ground swell of pro-draft propaganda, some of it from high places. Secretary of Defense Harold Brown, testifying concerning the return of the military draft, told the U. S. House Armed Services Committee that if the drafting of men is resumed, "we should include the registration of women." A few months later Gen. David C. Jones, chairman of the Joint Chiefs of Staff, told the Congresswomen's Caucus he would not object to the lifting of the prohibition against women in combat.

None of this is to say that a woman cannot be a good housewife and mother if she works, outside the home, even at a "man's job." I don't think there is any question, though, that a woman's holding a job increases the problems of fulfilling her traditional roles. And the alarming aspect of the woman's rush into the marketplace is that it is being promoted and used for sinister purposes that threaten the home and the future of the nation.

Women are paying the price for abandoning their traditional role. Succumbing to the unfamiliar pressures of their new unisex role, women are turning to crime in astonishing numbers, with armed robberies by females jumping 380 percent, fraud 480 percent, burglaries 289 percent, and larceny 465 percent in one five-year period during the seventies. Their new levels of anxiety and stress have brought on women the penalties that men have paid for climbing the ladder of wordly success—physical ailments ranging from mild maladies like insomnia to ulcers and heart attacks, increased smoking (and lung cancer), alcoholism, and drug addiction.

However, God is proving to have been an excellent engineer. When he designed the sex roles, he built a strong foundation and a rugged superstructure. Despite the best efforts of the feminist movement, a 1978 survey showed that 90 percent of the nation's wives still perform in the home in much the manner housewife-mothers have traditionally performed.

And here is the almost humorous evidence of the movement's failure to undo God's handiwork. A feminist author has found that even deeply committed feminists retreat to traditional ways of child-rearing in dealing with their sons out of fear that the boys may grow up to be "sissies."

Evidently, talking unisex is one thing but when it comes to significant males, even the feminist wants a man to be a man—and recognizes that that's something different from what a woman is.

In *Human Evolution* (University of Chicago Press, 1974), Dr. Bernard Campbell, University of California professor of anthropology writes:

> The human family is the simplest social unit with a complete division of labor between adult individuals. It is to the fact that the roles of man and woman are fully complementary that the family owes its continuance and stability. Any interchange of roles, such as we see today in Western society, could threaten that stability....

Christians, wake up! The attack against the role of housewife is an attack against God's design for the home.

MATE

"Romantic love is rapidly declining and perhaps moving toward extinction. There is a shift from sentiment to sensation and from longing to immediate gratification."

Prof. Marian Kinget of the University of Michigan

spoke these words to a meeting of psychiatrists, psychologists, and sociologists at a meeting in London, England, in 1979. She went on to say that the concept of romantic love is universal and that Western thought, in particular, regarded it as built into the sexes and unchangeable.

If romantic love seems to be ingrained in every culture, so much a part of human nature that it has been regarded as unchangeable, why is it now declining? Why is it moving toward extinction?

Professor Kinget answered that question. Romantic love, she said, is being killed by Women's Lib.

Thanks to the feminist movement, she explained, women have more freedom of thought and action because of the pill and contraceptives in general. Also, she said, the feminist campaign for equality has given women more independence in their financial, political, and personal lives. She reasoned that this has turned women away from "dreaming of moonlight and toward a more workable approach" to sexual relationships.

Though she emphasized that she was not a supporter of Women's Lib, the professor saw some hope that feminism could have a positive benefit by increasing mutual respect between the sexes. But her key observation is found in this sentence: "In its raw form, it (feminism) is destructive because it *deliberately* aims at making women, particularly housewives, feel that they should be discontent."

The emphasis on the word "deliberately" is mine. Women's Lib is calculatedly, purposefully striving to destroy the basic sexual relationship between men and women that forms the foundation for marriage and the home. Since romantic love is the sugar coating

46

of that relationship, it stands to reason that it would be one of the feminists' prime targets.

Let me acknowledge that romantic love is not the ideal love on which lasting marriages are built. Romantic love has been misunderstood, abused, and used as an instrument of exploitation by sinful man. To rely on it as the strength of a marriage is to court disaster.

However, that is not to say—as some well-meaning Christian counselors are doing, thus playing into the hands of the enemies of the home— that romantic love has no place in God's plan for the sexes. I definitely believe it does. I believe that in a marriage relationship between a man and woman who are committed to Christ and controlled by the Holy Spirit, romantic love is one of the greatest blessings God has ever granted. A marriage excluding it would be a bland and boring social contract.

Romantic love is the affectionate, the emotional aspect of love. It may involve sexual attraction, but it's more profound than that. It involves the total attraction that draws the sexes toward each other and causes them to want to form mutually fulfilling relationships. Romantic love was what Adam expressed when, after looking over all the animals God had created, he found no companion suitable for him. When God made Eve, Adam said: "At last! This is the one!" (Genesis 2:23, my paraphrase). Enemies of the home try to depict romantic love as a cultural or traditional legacy, but that couldn't be so. Adam had no culture. He had never seen a woman before he emitted that rapturous reaction to Eve's appearance!

Recognizing romantic love to be related to the total, God-created, male-female system of mutual attraction, enemies of the home are bent on destroying it. Their aim is sketched plainly enough in the following statement:

"We must destroy love. . . . Love promotes vulnerability, dependence, possessiveness, susceptibility to pain, and prevents the full development of woman's human potential by directing all her energies outward in the interest of others." —Women's Liberation, Notes from the Second Year.

The strategy for destruction of man-woman attraction takes in the broad range of feminist tactics for converting the wife into a competitor rather than a companion. In my counseling ministry, we find that many marriages deteriorate when the wife gets a job. She loses something of her image as a woman, in the eyes of her husband, and takes on a touch of the "worker" image. If she earns more than her husband or displays a haughty, independent attitude, the problem is compounded. The man's attraction is to a woman, not to a "professional person" and certainly not to a competitor whose success makes him feel inadequate in his God-given role as a provider.

But the feminists don't stop with this general approach to destroying the attraction between the sexes. They are making a frontal assault against it.

Code-words such as "male chauvinist pig" and "dirty old man" are used repeatedly in ways that cast the normal male attraction for the female in an unflattering light. I'm in no way defending sinful sexual advances by men or male "sexploitation" of women on the job. But feminist propaganda goes beyond condemning such misdirected sexual attraction and strikes at the attraction itself. It coaches women to be hostile toward the attraction. It strives to give men guilt feelings and causes them to suppress or try to deny the attraction women have for them.

Thus, any man who opens a door for a woman, thus revealing he sees her as "different" and favors her, is made to feel like a "male chauvinist pig." Any man who surrenders his seat on a public conveyance may be rewarded with the feminist glare reserved for "dirty old men."

A natural male reaction to this nonsense—though, again, inexcusable—is a degree of hostility toward women in every area of life. Some men may even respond with sexual violence. On the surface, these results might seem contrary to the announced goals of the feminists, since they seem to make the woman's lot more difficult and dangerous. Actually, they are just the results some feminists want. They substitute, in the attitudes between the sexes, repugnance for respect, antagonism for amour, and contention for companionship. The more vicious men become toward women the better the hard-core feminist likes it.

The feminists foster the idea that women, on the other hand, should be sexually free. In many instances their spokeswomen have translated freedom to mean aggression. Thus, even in the sexual relationship itself, women are urged to usurp the role of the man. The masculine partner has traditionally been the initiator of sexual activity. It confuses and annoys men to find women behaving as pursuers rather than the pursued. By nature, it is impossible for men to respond normally to such behavior because the behavior itself is not "normal," in the traditional sense of the word.

Feminists are not, however, simply encouraging wives to become aggressive and demanding in their relations with their husbands. They advocate permissiveness, seeking sexual satisfaction wherever it can be found. In this way, they make even the sexual relationship a competitive, challenging situation. Instead of a love relationship, it becomes a contest to determine which marriage partner performs best. It becomes a proving ground in which the husband must either show that he can meet his wife's physical needs or else she will exercise her "right" to seek satisfaction with another sex partner.

Speaking of this scrambling of the sex roles, George Gilder said in *Sexual Suicide*: "Such insidious rivalry will usually erode the foundations of love and subvert all the other values of honesty, spontaneity, and and trust. . . . "

He concluded:

Males always require a special arena of glorified achievement from which women are excluded. Their concern with sexual differentiation is obsessive. Men can be passive without grave psychological damage only if the women are passive also. Aggressive and competitive women, unconcerned with motherhood, produce more ruthless men—and a society so competitive that it disintegrates. . . .

Militant feminists lash out against any trace of contentment in the husband-wife relationship. Their aim is to stir discontent even in the hearts of women who are perfectly happy in their marriages. The goal is to convince the contented wife that she is being cheated or that she is somehow inferior because she is emotionally dependent on one man, her husband. Wives are told they should be enriching their lives through sexual experiences with other men.

Toni Tucci is representative of the many feminist authors who push this theme. In her book *The*

Butterfly Secret, she urges older women to take a young lover. Women, she says, are foolish to depend on the men they are married to for their security. "There is no security, no solution," she says. "Every marriage ends in divorce, desertion, or death, and usually it is the woman who is left." Therefore, she advises, women should "start preparing for those days now"—that is, while they are still living with their husbands. How? "Get out and live—it's the only life you've got."

The thought is spelled out even more clearly in *The Document,* a declaration of feminism:

> *Marriage has existed for the benefit of men and has been a legally sanctioned method of control over women. . . . The end of the institution of marriage is a necessary condition for the liberation of women. Therefore, it is important for us to encourage women to leave their husbands and not to live individually with men . . . We must work to destroy it (marriage).*

Some feminist propaganda seeks to convince women that they don't need men as mates at all. It maligns the male anatomy, asserting that women don't require intimacy with a man for sexual satisfaction. Some of it even extols self-stimulation as a means of relieving sexual tension far more convenient than relationships with men and all their attendant complications.

The other sexual alternative offered women by the feminist movement is female homosexuality. This, its advocates say, is the ultimate step to freedom from male dominance.

In *Lesbian Nation,* (published by Simon and Schuster, 1973) radical feminist Jill Johnston urged women to reject men totally. Men have oppressed women and, therefore, have become their natural enemies. For this reason, she said, "the continued collusion of any woman with any man is an event that retards the progress of woman supremacy."

Notice, her pronouncement shifts the goal of the woman's movement from mere equality with men to supremacy over men. Ms. Johnston goes on to say: "The totally woman committed woman, or lesbian, who shares this consciousness with other women, is the political nucleus of a woman's or lesbian state—a state that women cannot achieve by demand from the male bastion but only from within, from exclusive woman strength building its own institutions of self-support and identity . . ."

She then unwittingly acknowledges the God-ordained order of things and reveals that the Women's Lib movement represents direct defiance of God's plan, for she says: "The male remains the biological aggressor and as such [is] especially predisposed to take cultural-political advantage of the woman. It is against this advantage that feminism deploys itself."

Ramparts, one of the leading feminist propaganda pamphlets, carried an article by Marlene Dixon in the December 1969 issue, in which she wrote: "The institution of marriage is the chief vehicle for the perpetuation of the oppression of women; it is through the role of wife that the subjugation of women is maintained. . . . "

Martha Shelley in *Sisterhood is Powerful* said: "Lesbianism is one road to freedom—freedom from oppression by men. . . . Lesbianism involves love between women. Isn't love between equals healthier than sucking up to an oppressor?"

Many women who have joined the feminist movement because of its noble-sounding goals of equal pay and equal rights have not realized the significance of the movement's alliance with the lesbian cause. In a meeting of the National Women's Political Caucus in Boston in 1975, however, one member said:

> The (feminist) movement in the past has resisted having lesbians up front and, say, on the media or as an open presence, because they were so afraid that women would be afraid to come into the movement or that everybody would be labeled a lesbian, and I think that this has very much changed now. There is a very supportive atmosphere and a real sharing together. We're beginning to understand the issues, and how lesbianism really affects all women and all people, really.

Part of the feminist strategy to win acceptance for lesbianism, not just as an "alternative lifestyle" but as a weapon against male dominance, is to create the impression that this perverted behavior is already pervasive.

In his book *The Assault on the Family*, Dr. James M. Parsons describes one major effort that has been made to paint this false picture:

> In Houston, at the (IWY International Women's Year) conference, which was dominated by lesbian homosexuals, the claim was made by lesbians to newsmen that over five hundred lesbians were in attendance. Chants of "dyke, dyke, dyke" and the simultaneous release of balloons with the message, "We are everywhere," did not convince knowledgeable newsmen that over 150-200 lesbians were actually present. But

the psychology was obvious: Convince every-
one that homosexuality is rampant. . . .

For the true aims of Women's Lib, there is no better place to turn than to the acknowledged "mother" of the movement, Betty Friedan, who remains one of Lib's foremost theorists and propagandists. In *True* magazine she said:

You've heard, of course, that women's lib wants to destroy the family unit and take the pants off men. There is a lot of bitterness and rage exploding in women today. This rage, indeed, may temporarily turn a woman against the very husband, children, marriage, and home women were supposed to live for; and because she wants nothing to do with men, may even temporarily turn her off of sex.

Her use of the word "may," of course, is ridiculous. Ms. Friedan knows perfectly well that will be the result, or at least hopes it will be, since that is the goal of Women's Lib. She goes on, however, to an effort to exonerate Women's Lib from all blame for the mess it is causing:

The women's movement is not the cause of this exploding rage, but it may be the only hope for its cure. All this hostility is the symptom that something is terribly wrong with the way marriage, family, and home are structured right now—built around separate sexist poles, the obsolete and unequal roles women and men have been trying to play. . . .

The fault, then, according to Ms. Friedan, is in God's plan for the home and family. The solution? Simply do away with God's plan:

54

mothers. These women were presented in a most favorable light. They were described as smart, fun-loving go-getters who really knew how to enjoy life. "Other than not wanting children," the psychologist said, "they seemed like highly achieving, intelligent people who were not out of the ordinary in any other way."

These "perfectly normal" nonmothers were depicted as having no animosity toward motherhood. "They all saw motherhood as being a valuable, time-consuming, creative job that they thought they were not cut out for," the researcher said, adding: "Most had assumed they would have children. At some point in their 20s, all of them began to question this assumption, many of them because of involvement in their careers."

The findings of this study may be entirely valid. But its central message to potential mothers is that the smart, achieving woman, the one who is really "in," chooses a career over children.

It's true that some women shouldn't become mothers. They are not suited to nurturing children because they are too self-centered, rebellious, or downright sinful. The root reason is that, to be a good mother, a woman should be yielded to the control of the Holy Spirit, and many women are not.

However, the thrust of the subtle feminist propaganda, using selected truth as ammunition, is to encourage *all* women to shun child-bearing and opt for careers outside the home.

Of course, many women, simply because they are sexually active, have children without being committed to motherhood. To make it easy for these mothers to abandon their housewife-mother roles and enter the marketplace, the feminists have made child care one of their priority projects. The object of the push for government-funded child care is to give the unhappy mother—who may have been made unhappy by feminist propaganda—a solution to the "problem" that's keeping her in the home. Get the mother out of the home—that's the goal. A motherless home, they know, is a vulnerable target for their attack on the family.

In attacking motherhood, as in other areas of their broad-scale offensive, however, the feminists are not content with subtle and indirect tactics. They go for the jugular vein.

Simone de Beauvoir, one of the most forthright enemies of the home, has said: "No woman should be allowed to stay at home and raise her children. Women should not have the choice, precisely because if there is such a choice, too many women will make that one. It is a way of forcing women in a certain direction." (From *The Second Sex*, Knopf Publishers, 1953.)

Again, the best source of information on feminist strategy is the captain of the host, Gloria Steinem. In a lecture at Southern Methodist University in 1979, Ms. Steinem said:

"Only by keeping control of women's bodies, as a means for child production, can you make sure that racist systems will prevail. . . . We (women) are going to take control of our bodies. We are going to decide to have or not to have children. It will become a right as recognized as free speech."

Ms. Steinem makes it seem that someone is trying to force women to conceive and have children. That, of course, is absurd. All women in America's free society have a right not to become pregnant if they do not wish to. There are laws protecting them from being forced to submit to sexual intercourse and conception.

What Ms. Steinem was really arguing for was the right of women, after they have willingly submitted to intercourse and conceived, to terminate their pregnancies prematurely by abortion. In other words, she is saying that one solution to the "child problem" is simply to kill the children while they are still in the womb.

I am not implying that Ms. Steinem is a bloodthirsty freak who delights in the slaughter of innocent, unborn babies. Her aim is to "liberate" women from all their God-given roles. She probably has nothing against children except that they stand in the way of this aim. Killing them is simply a means to an end. And Ms. Steinem follows the familiar guideline of the ungodly: The end justifies the means.

In her SMU speech, she specifically identified the anti-abortion movement that has sprung up in reaction to the feminist pro-abortion lobby as one of the foes the Women's Lib movement would have to take on. She said:

> In spite of the Supreme Court decision upholding abortion on demand, we have to realize we will have to fight for the right to reproductive freedom many times. If we are controlled on our means of reproduction, we can't have any other freedoms.

The basic cause of women's oppression is that female bodies beget children, she said, explaining:

> The patriarchal system controls women through controlling reproduction and sex, and says that all sex is immoral unless directed at having children.

In that remark, Ms. Steinem reveals that she includes not only distortion and half-truth, but the outright lie, in her arsenal of weapons for destroying the home. Assuming that she uses "the patriarchal system" as a synonym for God's design for marriage and the home, nothing in that system says that sex is immoral unless its purpose is to produce children. God ordained sex as a wonderful means of expressing love and as part of his plan for the husband and wife to achieve oneness in the marriage relationship. At no time does God say sex in marriage is a sin when it is not intended to result in pregnancy, and Bible-believing Christians do not label it a sin.

Ms. Steinem is right in her next statement, though. She says:

> You find the same forces that are anti-abortion are also behind laws on the books prohibiting various sexual acts between heterosexuals, and prohibiting sex between people of the same gender.

She said she believes the women's movement should not separate itself from the homosexual rights movement because "gays" are actually fighting against the same oppression as women's libbers.

Praise God, some people *do* recognize that adultery, fornication, and homosexuality pose a threat to the family and the home! And praise God, some people are taking a stand for the laws against these things— laws that were put on the books when America was governed by a Christian consensus that adhered to biblical values and scriptural morality! Somebody had better go to bat for those laws, because the enemies of the family are doing everyting in their power to replace them with laws that are more to their liking. And in many instances they are using the tax money of Bible-believing Christians to get the job done.

The $5 million Congress appropriated for the International Women's Year is a case in point. This money was to be used partly for state IWY conferences held in the spring and summer of 1977 and partly to finance the national IWY conference in Houston in November. The state meetings were to be open to all. Sessions representing a cross section of American women were to adopt resolutions and elect delegates to the Houston conference. The result was to be a "consensus of women's concerns."

Financing IWY with tax dollars might have raised no questions if the project had followed that script. But it did not. The National IWY Commission, heavily weighted with feminists, created state commissions in their own image. Result: Conservative women were given little chance to be heard. The state conferences, in effect, became federally financed rallies promoting the goals of the Women's Lib movement.

The tone of the national conference, then, was predetermined. Because of the "railroading" at the state meetings and an additional 500 pro-Lib delegates appointed directly by the National IWY Commission, only 15 percent of the 2,000 voting delegates at Houston were conservatives. In the three days of the convention, conservative delegates were allowed a total of five minutes on the floor to speak against resolutions proposed by the feminist majority.

Predictably, this "rigged" convention adopted twenty-five of the twenty-six resolutions included in the National IWY Commission's "National Plan of

Action." The most important of these resolutions called for:

—Ratification of the ERA.

—"Reproductive freedom"—government funding for abortion on demand; sex-education programs in all schools, including elementary, and programs providing contraceptive information, birth-control devices, and abortion counseling, all without parental knowledge or consent.

—Federally funded "flexible hour" child-care centers, a twenty-four-hour care plan that would cost an estimated $25 billion.

—Social Security coverage for homemakers, which would impose an annual tax of hundreds of dollars on families of nonworking wives and mothers.

—A "sexual preference" act giving full legal rights to homosexuals and lesbians, including legalization of homosexual marriages, child-custody rights for homosexuals, and freedom to teach homosexuality as an "alternative lifestyle" in the public schools.

These resolutions read like a summary of the feminist-humanist movement's grand design for destroying the American family. Yet they were publicized in the official IWY report adopted at Houston. Thus, they gave state and national legislators, federal and state administrators, the courts, and the American public the impression that this is what a "consensus of American women" wants.

That is what the enemies of the family got out of IWY for our tax dollars. What did the friends of the family get? Five minutes on the stand, all of it under ridicule and duress, to defend God's values and his design for the home. They were not even allowed to present their minority report.

Radical elements are continually looking for opportunities to use the tax dollars of friends of the family to finance their anti-family activities. The National Gay Task Force campaign for "gay rights" is an example of such an effort.

To counteract Anita Bryant's "Save Our Children" endeavor, the NGTF launched a vigorous public-education drive titled "We Are Your Children." The group sought to run this national campaign with an expanded staff paid through a federal grant from the Comprehensive Employment Training Act (CETA). If the grant were approved, it would mean that tax money would be used to promote acceptance of homosexuality as a legitimate lifestyle.

That powerful elements in the feminist movement—which has already used tax dollars—support just such acceptance, there is no room for doubt. In a book compiled and edited by NGTF (*Our Right to Love: A Lesbian Resource Book*), Lib theorist Gloria Steinem says:

> . . . *The truth is that heterosexual feminists ourselves will remain male-identified and "man junkies" to some degree until we dare to kick the habit of identifying with, and being given our self-image by, the patriarchy. . . . Acting together with other women and becoming . . . female-identified is a very long and inevitable part of gaining the power to reach a humanistic society in which we can integrate female and male, black and white, as individual, equally powerful human beings.*

Betty Friedan gave the link between feminism and homosexuality quasi-official sanction at the Houston convention by publicly announcing that she was willing to include the fight for lesbian rights in the women's movement.

In view of the message God presents concerning the home and the mother's place in the home, it is hard to escape the feeling that the enemy the feminists are really striking at is God himself.

The Bible says young women should be taught "to be sober (responsible), to love their husbands, to love their children" (Titus 2:4).

Women's Lib teaches just the opposite. It entices them to be irresponsible with respect to their God-assigned roles in the home. It educates them to consider their husbands at best excess baggage, at worst cruel oppressors depriving them of their "human rights." It coaches them to regard children as problems to be avoided—by abortion where necessary—or, if unavoidable, to be shunted aside in favor of careers and "self-realization" projects.

THREE

TARGET: THE CHILD

In spite of everything enemies of the home have done to make fathers and mothers despise their offspring, children still occupy a warm spot in the hearts of most people. Even the clever propagandists of the feminist movement find it difficult to rip through the emotional barricades God has erected for the protection of the young.

Being fully aware of this fact, enemies of the home have made children one of the major targets of their attack.

The warfare being waged against the home through our children is of such scope, daring, and intensity that it almost defies adequate description. Evidence of it and the well laid plans of those behind it literally overflow the shelves of the nation's public libraries. The attack is blatantly trumpeted by all the mass media—radio, TV, newspapers, and magazines. It is highly visible in the curricula of our teacher training schools, in the professional journals read by teachers—and in many of the textbooks our children study at school.

Among the cleverest assaults leveled at children by enemies of the home has been the International Year of the Child program.

IYC began in 1974 as a suggestion by a representative of the community of Non-Governmental Organizations at a UNICEF Executive Board meeting. The proposal was referred to the Economic and Social Council, which asked the UN secretary general to submit to the 1976 General Assembly a report on measures for preparing and financing an international year of the child. On the basis of the report, the Economic and Social Council recommended that the year be proclaimed for 1979, and in December 1976, the General Assembly passed the resolution authorizing it.

In April 1978, President Carter, by executive order, affirmed 1979 as International Year of the Child in the United States. He also appointed a twenty-five member U. S. National Commission for the IYC. For the Commission membership he drew from social welfare and child care advocates, the liberal-dominated National Council of Churches, the American Civil Liberties Union, the Children's Defense Fund, and UNICEF.

Notably absent from the list of appointees were representatives of evangelical religious groups. In the Family Protection Report, Dr. Robert Billings, executive director of the National Christian Action Coalition in Washington, complained that the "Commission lacks someone who can articulate moral concerns for our children." He said a "practicing minister or rabbi from the pro-family ranks would have added a necessary element."

The caliber of the commission was thus a tipoff that IYC was unlikely to promote the best interests of children as Bible-believing Christians perceive those interests. The strongest clue to this fact, however, was in the IYC resolution itself.

This resolution was drafted, remember, by the Economic and Social Council of the UN. Beginning with its second paragraph, the document made clear that IYC had underlying purposes that were related only indirectly to plans for children. That paragraph referred to "programmes benefiting children *not only for the well being of the children, but also as part of broader efforts to accelerate economic and social progress."* (Italics mine.)

Subsequent paragraphs were riddled with references to "development and international economic cooperation," "services for children (as) a vital component of social and economic development . . . implemented by the cooperative efforts of the international and national communities," "to provide a framework for advocacy on behalf of children," "programmes for children (that would be) an integral part of economic and social development plans." The resolution also emphasized the importance of government involvement and intercession on the behalf of children. Article 8 expressed "the hope that *Governments*, non-governmental organizations and the public will respond generously with contributions to attain the objective of the International Year of the Child and, through the United Nations Children's Fund and other channels of external aid, to increase substantially the resources available for services benefiting children" (emphasis mine).

In pursuing these objectives, the IYC Commission, at a meeting in 1978, defined its purpose as being to:

—"Eliminate . . . discrimination against children."

—"Encourage . . . responsible self-expression."

—"Encourage attitudes supportive of cultural pluralism."

—"Promote understanding and appreciation of differing cultural and societal roles."

On first glance, these aims seem totally commendable. Given the known ideological leanings of many of those who formulated these goals, however, they invite suspicion. "Eliminating discrimination" against children could mean forbidding apartment managers to exclude couples with children—or preventing parents from disciplining their children. "Responsible self-expression" could mean stating an opinion in a classroom situation—or adopting a homosexual lifestyle. "Attitudes supportive of cultural pluralism" could mean appreciating the rich cultures of ethnic groups in the population—or acceptance of sexual perversion, immorality, pornography, and "alternatives" to God's plan for the family. "Promoting understanding and appreciation of differing cultural and societal roles" could mean any number of worthy pursuits. Or it could mean not only accepting the morally offensive lifestyles already mentioned but actually encouraging children to approve and adopt them.

Judging from many of the statements and movements developing under the IYC banner, most of the goals sought are of the type that concerned Christians would find objectionable.

Let me pause to acknowledge that not everyone who became involved in IYC is an enemy of the home. Many well-meaning people gave the program their full support without ever realizing that its motivations were misrepresented.

Once the program got under way, many concerned people participated—to whatever degree they were allowed to do so—in order to swing the effort away from its original purpose and prevent it from undermining the home and family. Primarily because of these countermeasures, IYC fell far short of the hopes its sponsors had for it. If more concerned citizens had turned out, well informed and determined, the program might actually have been converted into a child-benefiting event—though hardly of the type it was designed to be.

Exemplifying the confusion created by the non-

Christian sponsors of IYC was this letter to the editor, which appeared in my hometown newspaper, the Fort Worth *Star-Telegram*, on October 23, 1979:

> *The International Year of the Child 1979 was proclaimed by the United Nations. It is our responsibility as adults to protect the rights of children. Christians should set the example because they know the importance of a child.*
>
> *IYC has led the community in activities that have enriched many . . . But what puzzles me is when I read in the news that someone who says he is a Christian speaks out against IYC.*

IYC promoters and participants did, indeed, support many ideas that were right and good. At an IYC workshop in my area, for instance, Marie Oser, director of the Family Institute of Texas and Texas representative to the IYC, strongly urged attitudes and actions to strengthen the family. She was critical of persons who express concern for many other issues but show no concern with the state of the family. On October 28, 1979, the *Star-Telegram* quoted her as saying, "We talk about the SALT treaty and solving the energy shortage, but where are we in support of families? Do we have to go into a war before we take steps in our country to make family life more viable, more supportive?"

Of IYC she said she hoped its activities would "produce the things in our communities that say to our children, 'We care, you are important.'"

Neither I nor anyone knowing the importance the Bible places on children could quarrel with that statement.

Mrs. Oser went on to point out that the communities themselves should provide the approaches to strengthening the family and helping children to have better opportunities. "Ideas started in meetings like this become policy," she commented.

It's at that point that Christian citizens should have gone forward in force and presented their ideas about the home and family and the kind of activities that truly benefit children. The news story that told about Mrs. Oser's appearance gave no indication that anything of that nature occurred.

Mrs. Oser said, correctly, that in this country the government should not dictate how things should be done, that "we get together . . . and discuss ideas and then follow through with what the majority decides." She urged the audience not to let go of this participatory process, warning: "If you don't want government control in your lives, you have to get involved." She said she hopes the IYC commission's efforts will produce "a concrete commitment of local, state, and national level for activities that support our children and their families and improve their quality of life."

It would be hard to believe that the Mrs. Osers who supported IYC were anything but sincere in their concern for the family and the well-being of children. However, Mrs. Oser herself urged support for some IYC-backed legislation that Christian parents would view with considerable uneasiness. And, given the origins of IYC and the beliefs of many who would administer the programs it advocates, the very idea of the government being involved in anything to do with the home and with children is nothing less than frightening.

One opponent of the IYC approach put it this way:

The basic premise of the International Women's Year, and of the entire Women's Movement, is to look to a centralized government to solve the economic, social, physical, and emotional problems of women . . . Likewise, the premise undergirding the International Year of the Child is: it is the responsibility of all society (meaning the government) to fulfill the needs of children. So the reasoning that pervades the IYC meetings goes basically something like this: 1) "Here is a problem facing children." 2) "Let's formulate a program to solve it." 3) "How can we get the program funded?" The necessary conclusion of such reasoning must be intensified involvement of the federal government in family life.

The IYC opponent points out that control is the antithesis of freedom and warns:

While there is yet time, parents of the nation should give serious thought to the way they want to go. Do they want to retain freedom to rear their children, or do they want children to become the virtual wards of the State? It is not possible to have it both ways.

A look at some of the laws promoted in the guise of helping children reveals the cause of the deep concern expressed in that statement.

The Domestic Violence Prevention and Services Act (HR 2977) is an example of the laws I am talking about. Introduced by California Congressman George Miller, it sounds like a commendable bill. It allots $65 million "to provide for Federal support and stimulation of State, local, and community activities to prevent domestic violence and assist victims of domestic violence . . . The Secretary of HEW (will) serve as Coordinator." The measure would provide "a national clearinghouse on domestic violence . . . not less that three-quarters of such funds will be distributed in grants to private nonprofit organizations . . . particularly those operating shelters."

Presented in this manner, the bill has drawn support from many well-meaning citizens. Who in his right mind would not be against domestic violence? What good Christian would oppose a bill aimed at preventing domestic violence and aiding victims of such violence?

The wording of the bill fails, however, to spell out what "activities" the various state, local, and community entities might use to prevent domestic violence, and that just happens to be the most important question. For an answer, we can turn to proponents of the measure.

Dr. Murray Straus, director of Family Violence Research at the University of New Hampshire, suggests that one way to approach the problem would be to "gradually eliminate physical punishment as a mode of childrearing." He also proposes that we should "eliminate the husband as 'head of the family' from its continuing presence in the law, in religion . . . and family life."

These are not just the thoughts of one man. In 1974 the U. S. Commission on Civil Rights issued its official report on domestic violence, the report that gave impetus to the proposed legislation. Its summary of recommendations for preventing domestic violence includes 1) eliminating the husband as head of the house and 2) eliminating all physical discipline in the home.

The bill says only that it prohibits "a violent act, or threat of violence, that injures or may result in injury. The violence may occur between spouses, or former spouses, or between people who are or have been living together."

It does not say specifically that this includes children, but clearly it does. It does not say that a mother's paddling or a father's threat to spank a child could be regarded as "a violent act" or a "threat of violence," but persons familiar with the way legislative language can be interpreted warn that the bill could easily acquire that meaning through court decisions. This is especially believable in view of the known leanings of those supporting the legislation and the recommendations of the Commission on Civil Rights.

A resolution pending action in Congress at this writing would further insure court interpretation of the bill as a ban on physical discipline. Titled House Concurrent Resolution 109, it states that it shall be "the sense of Congress" that children possess certain fundamental rights. One of the rights listed is the right to be "free from psychological and physical abuse." The wording, again, is vague, but it clearly leaves open the possibility for paddling to be included under the ill-defined umbrella of "physical abuse." And such "sense of Congress" resolutions are most influential in helping judges arrive at interpretations of the law when cases go to trial.

References to religion by advocates of domestic violence laws are not to be taken lightly. The enemies of the home know perfectly well that the Bible commands parents to use physical correction to discipline their children, and they anticipate their strongest opposition coming from people with firm Christian convictions.

Christian parents, and others who believe child-rearing should be the responsibility of the home and not the government, must realize that the real motivation of many of those pushing this and other child-oriented laws is to take children away from the family and put them in the hands of the state. Failing this, the goal would be to see that the state, rather than the parents, has the dominant role in rearing children and determining their values.

Basically, the idea is simply to destroy God's plan for the home and family and substitute for it one devised by self-centered man and designed to serve his purposes.

One important point ignored or lightly dismissed by proponents of new domestic violence laws is that statutes already on the books prohibit genuine physical abuse of children or wife-beating and provide punishment for such behavior. The clearest evidence that backers of the new proposals want to undermine biblical teachings about child rearing has been provided by a federal law enacted in 1974.

The law defines child abuse in broad terms including "maltreatment" committed "under circumstances which indicate that the child's health or welfare is harmed or threatened." Under this law, each state receiving federal money under the program created by the law must have a state child abuse and neglect law. The state law must provide "for the reporting of known or suspected instances of child abuse or neglect."

All states now have laws complying with the federal law. The one adopted by my state, Texas, makes a person guilty of a misdemeanor crime "if the person has cause to believe that a child's physical or mental health or welfare has been or may be further adversely affected by abuse or neglect and knowingly fails to report."

The implications of this measure are extremely

disturbing to anyone nurtured in America's traditional freedoms.

The reporting required by the law, first of all, is to be done to the state's Department of Public Welfare, not to a law-enforcement agency. Second, the law tends to force every citizen to become a spy against his neighbor. Not only that, but the citizen-spy is to report not just what he actually sees but what he suspects. No punishment is provided against the person who makes a false report. But if something that can be defined as abuse occurs in your neighbor's home and it can be proved that you had reason to suspect it but failed to report it, you could, in my state, be charged with a crime.

And that's not all. Reports of child abuse made to the Department of Public Welfare go into a computer system with a nationwide hookup. Once a person's name is entered into the computer as a suspected child-abuser, it stays in the system until removed by court action. Before a court will order it removed, the accused person must prove he did not commit the alleged abuse.

Thus, not only do the federal child-abuse law and conforming state laws set up a nationwide system that encourages neighbor to spy against neighbor. They also violate the constitutional principle that accused persons are innocent until proved guilty. Under this system an accused person is guilty until he proves himself innocent. And the system operates under the auspices, not of duly constituted law-enforcement agencies, but branches of state and federal bureaucracy.

One might expect to encounter a system like this in Cuba or the Soviet Union, where government employs fear and suspicion to control an enslaved citizenry, but not in our free society. If we allow this approach to operate in the area of child abuse, it will spread to other aspects of life. It might well be the end of our freedom.

If any doubt remained concerning the true aims of those masterminding the IYC and the legislation ostensibly designed to protect children, the program called "A Child Health Plan for Raising a New Generation" would lay those doubts to rest.

The book outlining this plan was published in North Carolina in 1978. It consists of a report from the Joint Child Health Planning Task Force, which was formed by the North Carolina Department of Human Resources and that state's chapter of the American Academy of Pediatricians. A medical consultant of the U. S. Department of Health, Education, and Welfare set the study in motion by approaching the North Carolina Division of Health Services to prepare a plan to "regionalize child health care." The plan was to serve as a model for a national child health strategy.

The plan, purporting to "embrace all children," proposes programs that would provide, outside the home, all of the "variety of health services . . . needed by children at various ages." Services not considered essential at the community level would be provided on a regional basis.

The heart of the plan would be a "health care home." Notice the borrowing of the word "home" to make the plan more palatable to those who might sense in it a threat to the family and to parental authority. This "home-outside-the-home" would "provide or arrange for the services needed to maximize health as well as minimize illness."

Those last words are significant. The purpose of the plan is not merely to insure for children the absence of illness but the highest possible level of functioning and development—according to someone's standards. Who will decide what values determine those standards? You can be sure the state's planners do not envision the parents as being the ones to fulfill that role. The scope of the undertaking, as described in the book, is simply overwhelming. It takes in every aspect of life—"hygiene, nutrition, sexuality, safety, family life, parenting, and physical and mental development," "emotional, social, environmental and medical" factors involving the child's health, "vocational and educational counseling, personal counseling, and crisis support."

A key figure in the program is the "child advocate." An agent of the state, this individual would provide the surveillance needed to determine what "services" any given child might require. The advocate would be the enforcer, the one who would see that the standards set by the state for "health services" were met for all children. In the words of the plan itself, the advocate's service "includes social action on behalf of the rights of all children." To put it plainly, the advocate would be authorized to use the power of the state to force parents to let their children receive the prescribed "services," whatever those might be, or even to take the children out of their homes to administer these "services."

Parents who live by the biblical moral code would do well to delve into the nature of some of the "services" this plan would provide. They include:

—Family planning services—"including pregnancy testing, sex education, and contraceptives." These would be available "to all sexually active persons regardless of age." Assistance with abortion also would be provided.

—Help for the handicapped—"Handicaps may be physical, mental, emotional, or social." Judging from statements made by some supporters of this plan, belief in God might be regarded as a mental, emotional, or social "handicap." In IYC workshops in Houston, one "mental health care" advocate remarked that "50 percent of all children and youth are in need of some type of mental health services." And significantly, workshop leaders agreed that any parent who teaches a child about Jesus Christ or Christianity without presenting other religions is discriminating against the child by not allowing him to choose his own values. That points to another "service" the plan would provide.

—Health education—Under this benevolent-sounding heading fall such services as "values clarification, family life, and preparation for parenting" and "decision-making and self-actualization."

The most intriguing of these are "values clarification" and "self-actualization."

The methods recommended for "values clarification" are quite elaborate. A book by Simon, Howe, and Kirchenbaum, three humanist authors, presents seventy-nine strategies for performing this service for children. Room permits me only to sum up the objectives of these strategies. The goal is to shake the child free of values acquired from his home or community environment, particularly values related to religious belief, and to guide the child to create a value system of his own. The idea that each individual should develop his own system of values is a humanist concept. The meaning of humanism will be discussed in detail later. At this point I will say only that its teachings are contrary, and even hostile, to the Bible and to God.

In addition to "values clarification," the "health education" bracket embraces "mental health: e.g., stress, self-image, and lifestyle conflicts." This implies that there may be conflicts between parental values and "new lifestyles" the child may encounter in a world under the influence of humanism. No doubt there will be such conflicts. And planners have ways to resolve them. "Psychological testing and counseling may be appropriate," the plan says, "to assess and offset the effects of stressful life events on the emotional development of children." Evidently, children will be diagnosed as having mental health problems because of the values they absorb at home and then "deprogrammed." How else could the "stressful life events" caused by these "life-style conflicts" be "offset"?

—Home environment evaluation—If a child seems to have health or personal development problems, as described by the planners, the child's home can be subjected to an "evaluation." This is more than the proverbial camel's nose in the tent. It's Big Brother's foot in the door. Many homes have problems, and some of these problems deal misery to children. There's no denying that. But the answer to those problems is not to throw open the doors of all homes to government "evaluators." With agents of the government deciding which homes have problems, what standards will be used in determining the need for evaluation? The plan says such an evaluation can be justified by "suspected child abuse or neglect, nutritional problems, emotional trauma, or any one of many other clues."

In other words, a home could be slated for evaluation for any reason that might pop into the mind of a government functionary. If you believe in God and are teaching your children the Bible, that could be considered by some atheist health officer or social worker as grounds for an "evaluation"—a humiliating and intimidating invasion of the sanctity of your home.

—Day care—"We must strive . . . ," the plan says, "to develop sufficient day care arrangements that will ensure optimal growth and development." In the humanist dictionary, we know, "optimal development" would mean freeing the child from religious beliefs that might restrain him in his "self-actualization."

—Parenting education—This is recommended throughout the plan for all ages. The child health plan is related to International Year of the Child, and the International Planned Parenthood Federation has been designated as the agency charged with "Responsible Parenthood" programs for IYC. Presumably, then, Planned Parenthood would provide the guidelines for parenting education under the health plan. Planned Parenthood happens to be the world's leading proponent of abortion, sexual freedom and the providing of contraceptives "for all sexually active persons regardless of age."

—Genetic consultation—This puts the bold stamp of authoritarianism on the whole plan. Not only will this system probe your child's mind, your lifestyle, your home. It will even snoop into your genetic makeup with a view to deciding whether you or your children should be allowed to reproduce. The reasoning sounds innocuous enough. "For certain individuals, conception must be considered a risk to their health or that of the resulting children." But who decides who those individuals are? Who decides whether they should assume or reject the risks involved? If a nation is to remain free, those decisions must be left to the individual. When the state decides who shall be born and who shall not, freedom is gone.

You may be thinking you would simply refuse to cooperate in such a plan. Evidently, if the planners have their way, you will have no choice.

Under a description of responsibilities belonging to the child and the family, the plan says they "will accept one principal source of primary care" and "will make contact with that source often enough to provide continuity." The child and his parents "will arrange for examination, education, counseling, immunization, and other 'well child' services rather than only episodic treatment."

Notice the repetition of the word "will." There will be no options and no exceptions. And notice that these "services" are specifically *not* just for sick kids but also for the "well child."

In that case, you say, I will simply move to another state. But the planners are already a jump ahead of you. "Records will be transferred between health care homes in case of relocation," they note. And there will be no escaping across state lines. The principles of this plan have already been adopted as part of North Carolina's state law. Other states are under federal pressure to enact similar laws. And the plan calls for "follow up and tracking" that would keep the government's "health cops" on your trail no matter where you went.

I mentioned that there was a connection between the child health plan and the International Year of the Child. This is indicated by the fact that IYC logo is printed on the cover of the report and that the

National IYC Commission ordered copies of the book sent to all states as "an example" of things being done on behalf of children.

I also mentioned the influence of humanism that was evident in the plan. The IYC was promoted by many of the same humanist and humanist-oriented organizations and individuals who supported the International Women's Year. Thus, all three of these anti-home, anti-family, anti-God movements trace their roots to humanist thought and humanist activism. In the light of this fact, a close look at humanism seems imperative if we who believe in the home are to "know the enemy."

THE HUMANIST CONSPIRACY

Webster's New Collegiate Dictionary offers three definitions of the word "humanism":

"1 a: devotion to the humanities: literary culture; b: the revival of classical letters, individualistic and critical spirit, and emphasis on secular concerns characteristic of the Renaissance; 2: Humanitarianism 3: a doctrine, attitude of life centered on human interests or values; esp: a philosophy that asserts the dignity and worth of man and his capacity for self-realization through reason and that often rejects supernaturalism."

The third definition is the one that comes closest to describing the movement I have referred to in using the term "humanism." The proper term is "secular humanism." And the dictionary definition stops far short of a full explanation of the meaning of that term.

Humanism's chief spokesmen refer to it as a "faith" and a "religion." In one of its most important decisions, one too little appreciated by friends of the home, the

U. S. Supreme Court has defined humanism as a religion.

What are the tenets of this sinister religion? What do humanists believe and what causes do they promote?

The beliefs of humanism are set forth quite clearly in their two basic "statements of faith," Humanist Manifestos I and II. They are further articulated and amplified continuously in the American Humanist Association's magazine, *The Humanist*, and in assorted other publications of humanist organizations. The "bible" of the humanist cult is *The Philosophy of Humanism* by Corliss Lamont.

Some of the beliefs expounded in these writings reveal secular humanism to be:

—Atheistic: It denies the deity of God, the inspiration of the Bible, and divinity of Jesus Christ. It scoffs at such biblical concepts as the soul, life after death, salvation and damnation, heaven and hell. It rejects the biblical account of creation as a harmful myth.

Excerpts from humanist statements clearly set forth these beliefs as basic to the humanist creed. For example:

"We find insufficient evidence for belief in the existence of a supernatural; it is either meaningless or irrelevant to the question of the survival and fulfillment of the human race. As nontheists, we begin with humans not God, nature not deity."

"Religious humanists regard the universe as self-existing and not created."

"Humanists find that the traditional dualism of mind and body must be rejected." "There is no credible evidence that life survives the death of the body."

"Promises of immortal salvation or fear of eternal

damnation are both illusory and harmful." "Religious humanism considers the complete realization of human personality to be the end of man's life."

—Immoral: The humanists would hotly deny they are immoral, but, to Christians, rejection of God's moral absolutes constitutes immorality—and those absolutes the humanists definitely reject. These statements by humanist theorists reveal their attitudes on moral questions:

"Moral values derive their source from human experience. Ethics is autonomous and situational, needing no theological or ideological sanction."

"In the area of sexuality . . . individuals should be permitted to express their proclivities and pursue their lifestyles as they desire." ". . . Intolerant attitudes, often cultivated by orthodox religions and puritanical cultures, unduly repress sexual conduct."

—Disdainful of life: Humanists claim to be champions of the worth and dignity of man, but in their advocacies and actions they show no regard for the sanctity of life:

They support what they call " . . . the right to abortion . . . the right to die with dignity, euthanasia, and the right to suicide."

—Unisex: This position is not spelled out clearly in basic doctrinal statements, which only affirm: "Equality (of the sexes and) elimination of all discrimination based upon race, religion, sex, age, or national origin."

In the programs they support, however, the emphasis is clearly upon destroying the basic, God-ordained differences and relationships between the sexes, as I pointed out in discussions of the attacks against the husband-father and wife-mother.

—Socialistic: Humanism's doctrines are practically inseparable and indistinguishable from those of classical socialism. Humanist writers are forever finding facets of life in communist countries to tout as superior to the traditions of free nations, including America. Their creed states:

"Humanists demand a shared life in a shared world."

Notice that they do not simply ask, seek, or hope for it. They *demand* it. Does this not imply they will establish it by forceful overthrow of existing systems wherever possible, a procedure embraced by communism around the world?

—One-worlders: Humanists strive for a one-world community with no nationalistic divisions.

In their own words, their goal is to "transcend the limits of national sovereignty and to move toward the building of a world community."

The humanist endorses not only ideas that conflict with basic tenets of the Christian faith but also with the premises on which the American political and economic systems are based.

Humanism advocates equal distribution of America's wealth to reduce poverty and bring economic and social equality. Under such a system, people would no longer be rewarded for such traditional American qualities as initiative, perseverance, and thrift. The government—ultimately a world government—would control the distribution of wealth, power, and resources.

British author and outspoken Christian Malcolm Muggeridge summed up the fallacy of humanism beautifully in an article in HIS magazine, May 1973. He said:

> . . . *The most optimistic humanist would hesitate to suggest, in the light of his own and mankind's experience, that he is perfectible; but no such*

*inhibition arises when his extraordinarily cred-
ulous scientific mind envisages collective per-
fectibility . . .*

*It is often supposed that when people stop
believing in God they believe in nothing, but the
situation is far more serious. The truth is that
when they stop believing in God they believe in
anything . . . With that extraordinary credulity,
those who turn away from notions like the
incarnation are ready to accept without question the possibility of imperfect man creating a
perfect society.*

Are the values and goals of humanism of a kind that
Christians, or even morally decent nonbelievers, can
accept as the guiding principles for their lives and
their society? Certainly not! But these are the very
values and goals that are being imposed on every
individual and on society as a whole through the
political activism of a small but well-organized humanist minority.

Just how influential and effective the humanists are
in their brainwashing of the American populace is
nowhere more evident than in the nation's schools.
Humanist thought pervades public education like a
deadly venom from kindergarten through graduate
level. Its manipulation of the minds of children
through the schools constitutes one of the most daring
and dangerous attacks now being directed against
the American home.

At a public hearing conducted by a Governor's
Advisory Committee on Education in my home city,
Fort Worth, Texas, a strong contingent of parents
called for eliminating from public school curricula
everything but the basic subjects. Parents who testi-

fied overwhelmingly denounced much of what their children were being taught. The reporter who covered the hearing for a local newspaper said the parents were "railing against experimental courses that deal with nontraditional values."

Just what were these disturbed parents actually "railing" against? The newspaper account said they were protesting "humanism," "values clarification" and the basic assumption that "public schools exist for the sole purpose of social change."

These terms have been discussed briefly in earlier chapters. Now let's see how they manifest themselves in the attack on the home through the schools.

STRATEGY IN THE SCHOOLS

The broad strategy of the attack being waged through education is to alter the child's general outlook on life. This strategy is pursued by providing textbooks, literature, and other teaching materials that promote the humanistic philosophy. Such items permeate the American educational system.

One of the main thrusts in this assault on the conscience of the child is the already-mentioned "values clarification" approach. This is a cleverly calculated scheme to get the child to renounce the values he has learned at home and develop his own values. To encourage the child to make the change, the humanist material tries to convince the child that all values are of equal worth, that whatever values are *right for him* are *right, period*. He is taught that there are no absolutes, no such thing as right and wrong.

In choosing his value system, the child is urged to use a seven-step approach.

1. Choose the value freely—that is, without guid-

ance from any other source, whether parents, church, or society.

2. Make the choice from a set of alternatives—*including* those different from the values of parents, church, or society.

3. Make the choice after considering consequences—again, from the child's own understanding and without the help of parents, church, or society.

4. Be proud of the value chosen—because it is the child's very own, arrived at with the guidance of his own personal feelings.

5. Make the choice public and stand by it—be courageous enough to profess the value openly and influence peers to adopt it.

6. Act on the value—take steps to put the principle into practice.

7. Act on the value regularly—make it a part of a lifestyle that characterizes the child.

To even the semialert Christian, this approach waves a red warning flag at every step.

First, it's sheer nonsense to suggest that a child can choose values without any help from anyone. Since the usual sources of guidance are forbidden—parents, church, and community—the child is left at the mercy of the suggestions inherent in the humanistic approach itself. And what are those suggestions? Reject everything you've been taught by your parents, anything you may have heard in the church or read in the Bible, all that the traditions of your community hold to be proper conduct, and "do your own thing." Forget about right and wrong. Whatever you "feel" to be right for you is right.

The second step forces the child to think about values and lifestyles that it may not have occurred to him to consider. Attitudes about sex, for example, are crucial to the development of a value system on which to build a life. The predominant sexual orientation in the homes, churches and communities of America—and, thus, the one most children likely lean toward—is a heterosexual relationship between married adults. But Step 2 compels the child to ponder the alternatives? Homosexuality? Bisexuality? Autosexuality (masturbation)? Masochistic sexuality? Sadistic sexuality? Presumably, these are the "alternatives" that would have to be explained to the child to allow him or her to make a choice. And such explanations have actually been provided in some schools.

The story is told of one man who learned that his grandson's social studies teacher had presented a homosexual couple as guest lecturers in his classroom. They discussed the special problems they encountered in the community because of their lifestyle. The boy's father protested to the school's principal, but he was told to forget it. The principal said he saw nothing wrong with students getting a "modern view of life."

What's tragic about that story is that it's true—and that it's only one of thousands like it.

Step 3 appears on the surface to give the child a break. Just let him or her consider the consequences of his choice. When your children see the problems and miseries of the "alternatives" to God's way, they will choose the right values after all. But will they? Who is going to ensure that your child has the consequences explained fully and accurately? How, without proper guidance, can a child see far enough ahead and exercise sound enough judgment to make an intelligent decision?

The remaining four steps simply exhort the child to become aggressive, defiant, and determined to assert his self-chosen values and live his lifestyle no matter what others say or how adversely others may be affected. Assuming that some children, given power of humanistic suggestion, might choose values that conflict with those of their parents and the community, these steps constitute an incitement to rebellion against the home and the "establishment."

Under the "values clarification" method, the dynamics of the situation exerts immense pressures on the child to abandon previous values, wherever derived, and replace them with new ones. The system coaxes the child to lay bare his heart, mind, and soul before his teacher and his peers. In the discussion that follows, his personal convictions and feelings are subjected to comment and ridicule. If he is challenged, he must defend his values and the way in which he arrived at them. If his choice of values can be traced to parents, church, or any other source, it is automatically disqualified under the "rules of the game," which say the only valid values are self-chosen. This exposes the child who has been taught obedience and respect for parents to a cruel brand of intimidation. Skillful humanist teachers can manipulate discussions so as to make the peer pressure so intense that few young children are strong enough to adhere to their parent-taught values at all. Those who do can hardly escape feelings of shame and ostracism.

What issues are raised under the "values clarification" system for children to make value judgments about? The method has been applied to such questions as:

Premarital sex, extramarital sex, homosexuality, lesbianism, incest, women's lib, abortion, contraceptives, poverty, police brutality, racial equality, drugs, death, mercy killing, war, ecology, communism, free enterprise, disarmament, church, anger, fear, hate, love, marriage, divorce, family conflicts, parental values, interdependence (or world government), and a host of other topics.

- Standing alone, many of these matters would seem legitimate subjects for children to think about. In the humanist context of the "values clarification" approach, however, discussion of any of them could be manipulated to destroy traditional or Bible-based values.

To keep parents and other concerned citizens confused and impotent in their opposition to this attack on Christian values, the humanists play a continuing shell game with their strategies and materials. They constantly change the designations of their programs. Education in humanist values, for example, may be "values education," "valuing skills," "values clarification," or some fuzzier title like "self-awareness," "decision making," "self-acceptance," or "interpersonal relation skills." Films, textbooks, and other materials are disguised as opportunities for "open and honest discussion," but such discussion creates teacher and peer pressures that trained "change agents" (humanist teachers) can use to instill humanistic values. Often, the innocuous-appearing "discussions" are a camouflage for humanistic sex education, as even such basics as reading, history, and biology sometimes are.

Sex education in the public schools deserves the special attention of every Christian who is concerned about the attack against the home.

Earlier, I pointed out that the basic strategy of the feminist-humanist drive to destroy marriage, the home, and the family is to shatter the God-designed pattern for relations between the sexes and supplant it with a unisex society. Previous chapters were devoted to revealing how the enemies of the home are pursuing this goal by attacking the husband-father and the wife-mother.

As vicious and reprehensible as their tactics have been in attacking today's home, however, they are mild compared to those employed to attack tomorrow's home—through our children.

The primary weapon wielded for this purpose is "sex education" in the public schools. The success of this aspect of the enemy attack can be understood only in light of the "conditioning," or softening-up operation, that has been done on society as a whole.

As previously mentioned, every medium available has been used to program the American people to accept without a fight the revolution in sex attitudes sought by the enemy. Some of the most effective tools used for the purpose have been the popular syndicated "advice columnists." Many people read these shallow counselors "just for kicks," not realizing the cumulative effect their godless advice can have on their mentality. Many parents who might indeed be immune to the subtle persuasiveness of these columnists nevertheless, by openly reading them, set an example for their young children, who might not have the same powers of resistance.

Ann Landers, in advising mothers to put their daughters on "the pill" if they find out they are having premarital sex, justifies her position with a now-popular copout: They're already doing it anyway, and you'll only alienate them if you try to stop them. In one column, after giving such advice, she wrote: "And please, don't any of you out there write and clobber me for not advising the mother to give her daughter a lecture on morals. It's too late for that."

This echoes one of the most outrageous arguments the enemies of the home employ to undermine resistance to their demolition job. It says: "Go on and give up—the battle's a lost cause!"

That's a blatant lie. The battle is not lost. Young people are starving for guidance. Their God-given consciences scream out to them: "Stop! This is wrong! You're ruining your life! You're forfeiting your hope for future happiness!" But all they hear from the world is the evil urging to "do your own thing"—and from too many gullible parents and so-called Christian leaders the handwringing cry that "it's too late." To those who seek righteousness, it's never too late. God sees to that. For his mercy endureth forever (Psalm 138:8).

Ann Landers' twin sister "Dear Abby" told parents who had discovered their daughter was a lesbian to "accept her as she is and let her know it." How tragic! True, many parents slam the door to any possibility of helping their daughters by a harsh and unloving reaction to such discoveries. But girls with lesbian inclinations can be helped to a proper sex orientation if the problem is approached correctly. The advice columnist precludes any attempt at such help by simply denying that there's a problem.

Some of the most damnably devastating propaganda for sexual misorientation comes from the social scientists. Two sociologists, William A. Simon and John Y. Gagnon, reasoned in an article in *Today's Health,* April 1973, that sex is nothing but a form of play. They wrote:

"If sex is merely a form of play, then our concerns with who does it, how old they are, what their

marital status is (unless we are concerned with disease or pregnancy) is misplaced.

When sex is fun, it is subject to the morality of fun. It is entered into by choice and anyone may do whatever good manners dictate; the rules are made up by the partners. We may wish to restrict elders with children, but what objection do we have to older people teaching younger people about games or sport? Since play is nonconsequential, it is done with low emotional input by professionals whose livelihood depends on the activity. There is an interest in skill, but only to improve the content of the game itself.

Thus, the expression of love that God established to be the foundation of marriage and the home is degraded to the level of a sport. Even lower than a sport, in fact, because every sport at least is governed by a fixed set of rules. The sex sport, in the minds of these sociologists, has none.

Simon and Gagnon go on to describe sex as a private matter, something that concerns only the participants and is nobody else's business:

It is apparent that the psychosocial changes necessary to alter the process will not affect all sectors of the population at the same time or penetrate them at the same rate.

The major pattern of change will be the softening of gender identity lines. It will take most of its force early in life by more strongly curbing aggression among males, an increased dressing alike among children, and patterns of child rearing in which the occupational dimension of male life is nearly totally removed from the life of the child (emphasis mine).

Such thought-shaping writings have been a moving force behind "the softening of gender identity lines" occurring in sex-education programs. They have also contributed immensely to the "softening up" of an unsuspecting society to accept "new" and "different" ideas about sex—and permit these ideas to be taught in the schools.

These two sociologists go on to advise us:

> It is our expectation that young people in the future will be more sexually active than their parents or even any generations over thirty in 1970. These changes will be relatively slow in occurrence, and increases in the proportions of the sexually active will be smooth and not eruptive in character. Toward the end of this 25-year period, there will begin to be a steady increase in sexual activity among young people under 16, and general increases in erotic behavior during early adolescence.

Sociologists and other worldly thought leaders have done much to help fulfill their own prophesies. By continually glorifying sexual permissiveness and predicting increased premarital sex, they have contributed to the "everybody's doing it" atmosphere that has encouraged millions of young people to engage in sex sin.

As one psychoanalyst put it (they're not all in league with the home wreckers), "The prevailing attitude is that virginity is something a girl must 'get rid of.'" This psychiatrist, Dr. Natalie Shainess of New York, says this is destructive to a young woman.

A physician, writing in a medical journal, said that "the girl who doesn't want to 'go all the way' before marriage is considered ridiculously puritanical not only by her peers, but also by her professors." He went on to say that a girl is pressured from every side to "' free' herself of her 'inhibitions.'"

He spoke primarily of the situation existing in colleges. Now, with sex education and the more subtle "change guidance" offered in schools, the intimidation of girls to make them receptive to sexual activity begins much earlier—as early as kindergarten!

The physician, Dr. Charles Millard of the Rhode Island State Health Department, pointed directly at the "softening up" work being carried out through the media by enemies of the home:

> The inundation of the public—via newspapers, magazines, radio, and TV—with stories and articles with marked emphasis on sex, sexual freedom, and the advocacy of new sexual mores is apparent to even the casual observer. All of these factors, plus peer pressure, are subjecting these young people to an unfair and unjust psychological assault.

And if the assault is unfair and unjust to college-age young people, how about high schoolers, elementary school children, and preschoolers!

"All in the Family," long one of the nation's most watched TV entertainment programs, has provided some of the most loathsome examples of how the enemies of the home use television in their softening-up operation.

In one episode, the obvious goal was to sell the public on lesbianism as an acceptable "alternative" life-style. It would be impossible to pull off a coup like that with a direct sales pitch. Knowing this, the writers sneaked up from the blind side. They let their lesbian be a beloved aunt of Edith, Archie Bunker's wife. The aunt dies. At her funeral, Edith bumps into her unmarried aunt's roommate. In the blubbering conversation that follows, the roommate reveals that she and the aunt were lesbian lovers.

Edith, though dutifully shocked, has to be sympathetic. What else could she be in the presence of a grief-stricken person and under the influence of her own grief for her aunt?

And, of course, Edith carries much of the audience right along with her. If Edith, steeped as she is in "old-fashioned" morals and traditions, can switch to a more receptive attitude toward lesbianism, who but an insensitive monster could resist?

The writers hope that viewers won't notice how their emotions—their feelings of awe and mourning over death—have been used to manipulate their thinking about a totally unrelated issue.

Another episode of "All in the Family" used a similar gimmick to promote acceptance of male homosexuality. Again the direct sales approach was shunned in favor of a play on the emotions. The homosexual in this instance was a blind boy. You might not approve of homosexuality, but how could anyone "be mean" to a poor, pitiful blind boy?

In sports, where there are rules, both of these attempts to grease the skids of public opinion with emotions of sympathy would be called "cheap shots." They are representative, though, of the unscrupulous and totally unfair tactics used by enemies of the home to "condition" the American people to accept their ideas—and to make all who resist seem ignorant, old-fashioned, and unfeeling.

CHILDREN'S RIGHTS

The noble concept of human rights also has become a favorite tool of the home wreckers. Civil rights won the attention and the support of most Americans during the struggle of the nation's black minority for equal political and economic opportunity. The feminists and the homosexuals have tried to ride the coattails of the rights movement, as I have previously noted. But the enemies of the home have carried the "rights" cause an astonishing step further. They have launched a crusade for what they call "the rights of children."

On the surface, this offensive against psychological and social child abuse seems altogether pure and noble. But close examination reveals it to be nothing less than a cover for a movement to take children away from their parents, at least ideologically, and impose on them the atheistic thought patterns of secular humanism.

Any doubt that this is the actual motive can be eradicated by reading what the humanists themselves have to say on the issue. For instance, the March 1974 issue of *MS. Magazine* printed this version of "A Child's Bill of Rights," written by humanist theoretician Richard Farson:

1. The Right to Self-Determination. Children should have the right to decide the matters which affect them most directly. This is the basic right upon which all others depend. Children are now treated as the private property of their parents on the assumption that it is the parents' right and responsibility to control the life of the child. The achievement of children's rights, however, would reduce the need for this control and bring about an end to the double

standard of morals and behavior for adults and children.

2. The Right to Alternative Home Environments. Self-determining children should be able to choose from among a variety of arrangments: residences operated by children, child-exchange programs, 24-hour child-care centers, various kinds of schools and employment opportunities. Parents are not always good for their children—some people estimate that as many as 4 million children are abused annually in the United States, for instance, and that a half million children run away each year. It should be noted that these are 1974 statistics.

3. The Right to Responsive Design. Society must accommodate itself to children's size and to their need for safe space. To keep them in their place, we now force children to cope with a world that is either not built to fit them, or is actually designed against them. If the environment were less dangerous for children, there would be less need for constant control and supervision of children by adults.

4. The Right to Information. A child must have the right to all information ordinarily available to adults—including, and perhaps especially, information that makes adults uncomfortable.

5. The Right to Educate Oneself. Children should be free to design their own education, choosing from among many options the kinds of learning experiences they want, including the option not to attend any kind of school. Compulsory education must be abolished because the enforced threatening quality of education in America has taught children to hate school, to hate the subject matter, and, tragically, to hate themselves. Children are programmed, tracked, and certified in a

process of stamping out standardized educated products acceptable to the university, military, business and industry, and community. Education can change only through the achievement of new rights for those exploited and oppressed by it—the children themselves.

6. The Right to Freedom from Physical Punishment. Children should live free of physical threat from those who are larger and more powerful than they. Corporal punishment is used impulsively and cruelly in the home, arbitrarily in the school, and sadistically in penal institutions. It does not belong in our repertoire of responses to children.

7. The Right to Sexual Freedom. Children should have the right to conduct their sexual lives with no more restriction than adults. Sexual freedom for children must include the right to information about sex, the right to nonsexist education, and the right to all sexual activities that are legal among consenting adults. In fact, children will be best protected from sexual abuse when they have the right to refuse—but they are now trained not to refuse adults, to accept all forms of physical affection, and to mistrust their own reactions to people. They are denied any information about their own sexuality or that of others. We keep them innocent and ignorant and then worry that they will not be able to resist sexual approaches.

8. The Right to Economic Power. Children should have the right to work, to acquire and manage money, to receive equal pay for equal work, to choose trade apprenticeship as an alternative to school, to gain promotion to leadership positions, to own property, to develop a credit record, to enter into binding contracts, to engage in enterprise, to obtain guaranteed support

apart from the family, to achieve financial independence.

9. The Right to Political Power. Children should have the vote and be included in the decision-making process. Eighty million children in the United States need the right to vote because adults do not vote in their behalf. At present they are no one's constituency and legislation reflects that lack of representation. To become a constituency they must have the right to vote.

10. The Right to Justice. Children must have the guarantee of a fair trial with due process of law, an advocate to protect their rights against the parents as well as the system, and a uniform standard of detention. Every year a million children get into trouble with the law. One out of every nine children will go through the juvenile court system before the age of 18. At any given time about one hundred thousand children are in some kind of jail. Some are held illegally, many have not committed any kind of crime, most have done nothing that would be considered a crime if done by an adult, and none has been given a fair trial with due process of law. The juvenile system was designed to protect children from the harsh treatment of the adult justice system—but it is more unfair, more arbitrary, and more cruel.

What makes Farson's "Bill of Rights for Children" so significant is that it apparently has the support of feminist leaders and a large segment of the Women's Lib movement. The political clout of these militant individuals and groups could force children's rights legislation through Congress and state legislatures. Feminist pressure is already preparing the way for such a legal gambit. This move has taken the form of a proposed House Concurrent Resolution. Introduced in the first session of the 96th Congress, HCR 109 asserts that its purpose is:

> To express the sense of the Congress that children possess both fundamental human rights and rights attributable to their status as children, and to call for the enactment of Federal and State laws to implement such rights to the fullest extent possible and to grant children additional rights equivalent to the rights now possessed only by adults.

The proposal goes on to say: "Resolved by the House of Representatives (the Senate concurring), that (a) it is the sense of the Congress that each child possesses fundamental human rights (and) (b) rights based on the needs of the child as a child. . . . " It lists under "a" and "b" essentially the same rights as those enumerated by Farson, though the wording is different. The resolution then states:

> It is the sense of the Congress that the United States and the several States should enact laws with respect to the children living within their jurisdiction that will (1) implement to the fullest extent possible the rights described in the first section of this resolution, and (2) ensure that such children may exercise rights equivalent to the rights that now may be exercised under Federal and State laws only by adults, except to the extent that any such right, if exercised, would detrimentally affect efforts to satisfy needs unique to children.

A concurrent resolution does not have the force of law, but the approval of HCR 109—which may have come to pass since this was written—would be a major victory for enemies of the home. Since an HCR forms the basis for future law, HCR 109 would point Congress in the direction of a full implementation of the so-called children's bill of rights. HCRs also are used in court to guide judges in determinations concerning the "intent" of legislation passed by Congress. Thus, in court tests of any laws pertaining to children's rights, the verdict would, thanks to HCR 109, be prejudiced in favor of the feminist point of view.

As further insurance against unfavorable court rulings in children's rights cases, the feminists are constantly promoting the appointment of judges with a bias toward Women's Lib. Can such things actually happen? The answer is a resounding "yes."

President Jimmy Carter appointed Assistant Attorney Patricia Wald to the Second Circuit Court of the District of Columbia. In 1974, Ms. Wald wrote, in an article in *Human Rights:*

> *The institution of childhood has been called the last legal relic of feudalism.*
>
> *Age should no longer be a bar to retaining and using one's own money, making valid purchases and contracts.*
>
> *An adolescent youth ought also to be able to seek medical or psychiatric care on his own . . . This option, of course, will become economically feasible only when national health insurance or alternative health insurance programs make provisions for vesting rights to engage such services in youth rather than parents.*
>
> *In situations where the interests of the child (no matter what his age) and the parents are apt*

*to conflict or a serious adverse impact on the
child is likely to be the consequence of unilateral
parental action, it is now argued that the child's
interests deserve representation by an independent advocate before a neutral decision maker.*

At this writing, rumor has it that Ms. Ward is being
groomed for appointment to the U. S. Supreme Court.

What would be so terrible about giving legal
recognition to the children's rights proclaimed by
Farson and promoted by the feminists?

It's hardly necessary to go beyond the first "right"
stated to see the possibilities for serious problems.
The "Right to Self-Determination." How does a child,
with his or her immature judgment and lack of
reliable data, make the weighty decisions concerning
"matters which affect them most directly"?

Or take the second one, "The Right to Alternative
Home Environments." What alternatives? Proposed
by whom? How could a child make an intelligent
choice about such a matter?

"The Right to Information . . . including, and perhaps
especially, information that makes adults uncomfortable." Would it be beneficial to children to have all
information about everything? What would they do
with all this information if they had it? What information did Farson have in mind when he said "especially
information that makes adults uncomfortable"? Why
would children "especially" have a right to that information, whatever it might be?

"The Right to Educate Oneself" is so ludicrous it
deserves no comment. "The Right to Freedom from
Physical Punishment" directly contradicts scriptural
principles of child rearing. The rights to political and
economic power make little sense considering that

children do not have the knowledge or judgment to exercise either. "The Right to Justice" provides an instrument for children, under who-knows-what influence, to use in legal warfare against their parents.

That leaves only "right" No. 7, "The Right to Sexual Freedom." It asserts: "Children should have the right to conduct their sexual lives with no more restriction than adults." That would bar parents from teaching their children the biblical truths about their sexuality and the God-ordained pattern for sexual morality, marriage, and the family.

"Sexual freedom for children must include the right to information about sex, the right to nonsexist education, and the right to all sexual activities that are legal among consenting adults," the elaboration on "right" No. 7 continues. Presumably, this would remove the right of parents to prevent anyone's teaching their children anything about sex, providing a legal foundation for public school sex-education programs that push children toward sexual permissiveness and even perversion. It would also establish a legal basis for the unisex education promoted by enemies of the home to eradicate male and female sexual distinctives. Finally, it would prevent parents from interfering with—perhaps even from counseling against—immoral, emotionally damaging, life-destroying sexual activities in which their children might become involved.

The enemies of God's plan for the family are well along in scheming to get unscriptural and perverted lifestyles taught in the schools. Lesbian Jean O'Leary, an official of the National Gay Task Force, said in an article titled "Struggle to End Sex Bias in the Public Schools": "School counselors should be required to take courses in which . . . a positive view of lesbianism is presented . . . [and] students . . . encouraged to explore alternate lifestyles, including lesbianism. . . . Schools (should) set up lesbian studies . . . use of lesbian books should be encouraged . . . Lesbian clubs should be set up in schools." The article was published by the New York chapter of the National Organization for Women (NOW).

Laws establishing the principles of the Children's Bill of Rights could deprive Christian parents, or others who object to their children's being taught promiscuous or unnatural sex, of any legal basis for a protest against such instruction in public schools.

Even without the legal protection of such laws, however, the enemies of the home are busily doing, in many communities, just what these laws would legally sanction. How can they get away with pursuing their home-wrecking goals even without the laws they are pushing? Because all the talk about children's rights, the emphasis given child abuse by the mass media and the weakening of marriage and the family under the attacks already discussed have softened up public opinion to accept things that once would have been regarded as outrageous. Children's rights and sexual freedom have been made to seem smart. They are what is "in." Anyone who objects to these things, in the public schools or elsewhere, is labeled either ignorant, old-fashioned, or a religious fanatic. To a frightening degree, the enemies of the home have used the familiar tactics of the big lie, character assassination, and intimidation to disarm the opposition.

The issue of sex education in the schools is further clouded in the minds of many unwary parents by the term "sex education" itself. The term leaves the impression that such courses teach youngsters about human reproduction, sexual hygiene, the dangers of venereal disease, and, perhaps, contraception. This is not the sum of subject matter taught in many such courses, nor is it the goal of many sex-education promoters merely to inform children in these areas. In fact, sex-ed advocates normally refer contemptuously to courses confined to these subjects as "plumbing courses."

In the booklet *Assault on the Family*, published in Melbourne, Florida, by Pro Media in 1979, Dr. John M. Parsons says that you can understand the real objectives of sex education only by a study of the publications of the sex educators. The sex-ed promoters have organized themselves into groups—the Sex Information and Education Council of the U. S. (SIECUS), the Planned Parenthood-World Population group, the American Sex Educators, Counselors, and Therapists (AASECT), and humanist groups calling themselves "Social Hygiene" or "Social Health" groups. Parsons notes that a small handful of writers produce most of the publications distributed by these groups, that these writers are all humanists, and all expound humanist goals in sex education as in all other facets of life.

As a result, sex education often incorporates recognizable humanist ideas: Homosexuality an acceptable "alternative"; abortion a method of birth control and a "right" of every girl and woman; pornography an aid to better sexual relationships through stimulation of activity; and the general theory that the best way to learn sex is to practice it whenever and with whomever you wish.

In short, sex education in its usual humanist-inspired form is simply another weapon used by the enemies of the home to destroy the family and reshape society after their own model.

To know this is simply to read what the promoters of humanist sex education themselves have to say:

"Students will thus be encouraged to explore alternate lifestyles, including lesbianism . . . The names and phone numbers of gay (homosexual) counseling services should be made available to all students and school psychologists . . . No school counselor should ever refer a student to a psychotherapist for the purpose of changing her/his sexual preference from gay (homosexual) to straight. Such conditioning conveys to the student that her/his feelings of love are unworthy and unacceptable; it causes immeasurable conflict and ego damage, and can never be done in the name of mental health"—From NOW sources.

"The American family structure produces mentally ill children"—Ashley Montagu, SIECUS-recommended author, to a convention of home economics teachers.

"I don't think the women's movement as such is going to remain a women's movement. I think . . . we'll stop describing ourselves as feminists and begin describing ourselves as humanists and really begin to deal with problems of creating a different kind of society"—Toni Carabillo, outgoing vice president of NOW, 1974.

"For the sake of those who wish to live in equal partnership, we have to abolish and reform the institution of marriage"—Gloria Steinem, editor of *MS. magazine.*

And, of special interest to Christians, Ms. Steinem also said (*Saturday Review of Education,* March 1973):

"By the year 2000 we will, I hope, raise our children to believe in human potential, not God."

These are the people who want to mold and shape the society of the future. These are the ideas being forced on your children in many of the public schools of America.

Anyone with a trace of discernment should be able to detect the strategy of the enemies of the home in pushing children's rights and sex education in the schools. It is not to benefit the children but to wrest the children from the influence of their parents and make them subject to the godless teachings of humanism. It is Hansel and Gretel all over again. The wicked witch is executing an evil plot to lure our children to her fascinating gingerbread house of adult rights and sexual "freedom," where she will have complete control over them. But this is no fairy tale. And if she succeeds in stealing just one generation of our young, she may have captured our whole society for many generations to come.

What would the "new society" really be like? Probably it would be a study in collective emotional disturbance. Dr. Parsons, previously quoted, notes that feminists are demanding sex education from kindergarten through twelfth grade. Of the possible effects of such a program, he says that an important factor in character formation and emotional development is "freedom from stimuli which thrust upon a child's consciousness the necessity of dealing with matters far beyond the child's age, or which demand mechanisms of self-control which the child has not yet developed." He explains:

> There is . . . a period of sexual latency in childhood, from about age five until puberty, when the normal child represses sexual thoughts, while the business of personal idealism, identification with significant adults, and studies in school proceeds. This allows for orderly forma-

tion of character, because the child's repression of sexual matters serves the purpose of developing self-control, by keeping sexually stimulating thoughts out of consciousness. That which interferes with the latency period interferes with the learning process, with discipline and self-control in school, and disrupts family life at home. An undisturbed latency period is definitely conducive to a healthy childhood, and the development of sound character.

Don't miss the irony of this situation. The humanists who accuse the traditional and scriptural home of producing mentally ill children are going to create a nation of mentally ill people. It seems to me there is ample reason to believe they have already moved a considerable distance in the direction.

DECEPTION IN "PARENTING"

For sheer stealth, nothing in the anti-home arsenal outranks the humanist emphasis on "parenting." A feminist writer in "Impact ERA" puts the term in proper perspective. She says:

> As in other roles now segregated by sex, I believe that fathering and mothering will converge more and more into "parenting," a word already in use by a number of child psychologists. Parenting will combine fathering and mothering into a single role in which the gender of the parent is largely irrelevant.

Notice the unisex implications, the goal of changing traditional roles and altering the basic structure of the institution of the family.

But changing the ideas of adults about "parenting," after they have already been "tainted" by tradition and their own upbringing, would be difficult and not very productive. The enemies of the home are fully aware of this fact. They're aiming their best efforts at the area that promises the greatest results. Again, the target is our children.

Courses in parenting are being taught now in many high schools across the country. Promoters of these courses want them worked down into the elementary levels as well.

Parenting course materials often quote two sources, Dr. Urie Bronfenbrenner and Dr. Jerone Bruner. Bruner is one of the developers of "Man: A Course of Study," an elementary grade curriculum now largely discredited because of its brazen humanist and one-world orientation. Bronfenbrenner is a student of Soviet society, having made several trips to Russia, and has been active in development of child-care systems modeled after those in the communist state. This should be a tipoff of the character of these parenting courses.

One titled "A Parenting Course for High School Students: Behavior Modification Communication" by Barbara Pruitt is widely offered and may be considered typical of those promoted by the enemies of the home. It follows the humanist-inspired model Parenting Program originally pushed by the Department of Health, Education, and Welfare. Leaning heavily on "Parenting Effectiveness Training" (P.E.T.) by Thomas Gordon, it stresses the familiar humanist goals: Break students from tradition, turn them against the values of their parents, subtly persuade them to adopt humanist values, and, ultimately, use the newly brainwashed generation to bring about the desired "social change."

Acknowledging that his program "differs dramatically from tradition," the author of P.E.T. advises that punishment is to be "discarded forever in disciplining children . . . all kinds of punishment, not just the physical kind." This emphasis in itself promotes one major goal of the home wreckers—that of alienating children of Christian homes from parents who follow biblical principles of child rearing.

The material blames parents for the problems children encounter in growing up and encourages children to defy their parents by justifying such rebellion. "They (children) only rebel against certain destructive methods of discipline (methods involving punishment) almost universally employed by parents," it says. Also: "Students will be able to understand how parents contribute to their children's behavior problems."

The curriculum is filled with leading questions and answers designed to shape the basic thought patterns of the student, not simply to instill knowledge about how to rear children.

Examples:

—On the "Social Maturity Test," students score points only if they select, out of four choices, the answer that they would *prefer* to live next door to a foreigner. Of course, socially mature persons should be able to live peaceably and happily next door to someone of their own or another nationality. But why should "social maturity" *require* someone to *prefer* to live by a foreigner? The answer makes sense only in the context of humanist one-worldism.

—In instructions to their test, students are told there are "no right or wrong answers" to such statements as:

—Living in a family group is the best way for people to live."

—"Teenagers should not talk back to parents."

—"Parents should not make children do things that are good for them."

—"A teenager should do what his parents want rather than what his friends want."

—"A child should obey his parents without question."

—"A boy should not try to be like his father."

—"Teenagers should learn from persons outside the family how to be good husbands and wives."

—"If a father loses his job, it is up to the community to help the family."

—"Sometimes children have a right to be ashamed of parents."

—"The father's employer or the government should help the father save for the future."

—"Families are happier if the parents come from families which are alike."

These statements are cunningly phrased to elicit thoughtful "yes-and-no" answers in the minds of students. Coupled with the instructions that there are no "yes" or "no" answers, however, these statements produce an anti-parent impact. They are calculated to create a question in the student's mind about the wisdom or necessity of obeying his parents and, in most instances, to put the student in direct conflict with his parents' values and child-rearing methods.

If it were a course to be taught to parents, this parenting course might have some merit. Designed to be taught to youngsters of high school age and below, however, it can be seen as nothing but a device for alienating children from their parents. It could serve a good purpose, for example, to instruct parents not to "exhort, moralize, preach" to their children on the grounds that these methods tend to be self-defeating in the process of molding character and enforcing discipline. But the matter acquires an entirely different complexion when an authority figure (a course of study) outside the home tells children their parents should not do such things. The parenting course in question repeatedly tells children parents should not do this or that. They should not "warn, admonish, threaten." They should not advise, give solutions or suggestions; this would be telling the child how to solve a problem. They should not lecture, teach, or give logical arguments. In doing so they would be trying to influence the child with facts, arguments, logic, information, or the parents' own opinion.

Children also are told that parents should not judge, criticize, disagree with, or blame their children. They should not make a negative judgment or evaluation of a child. They also should avoid probing, questioning, and interrogating in an effort to find reasons, motives, or causes for their children's behavior.

These are all things that most parents do from time to time, and with good reason, in rearing their children. It is difficult, in fact, to see how any child rearing could take place without use of some or all of these tactics when the occasion called for them. But the course—taught to children, remember—forbids them all.

The principal statement this course makes to children, then, is that almost everything their parents are doing is wrong. It tells them that when they grow up and become parents, they should not be the kind of parents their parents are.

In telling youngsters this, the parenting courses

foster rebellion and disobedience on the part of young people, defiance of the primary authority figures in their lives, and the breakdown of order, not only in the home but in the whole society.

This is the "social change" the humanist tactics promise to bring about. And if anyone doubts the effectiveness of their methods, let him look around. America abounds with evidence that their assault against the home and the traditional structures of society are working amazingly well.

Discipline has faltered to the point that many young people can go through our schools without learning to read and write. Order and respect for authority have so deteriorated that efforts at law-enforcement are all but futile. With serious crimes increasing 200 percent or more in two decades, prisons can't be built large enough to hold those convicted of crime, and penal systems in much of the country are forced to cut back rehabilitation efforts and get offenders out of custody and back into the streets as quickly as possible.

Unless decent people, primarily Christians, stand and repel this enemy onslaught on the home, its success will snowball in the next generation. For today's young are being taught not only how to rebel against *their* parents, but also how to ensure that their own children will rebel against *them*.

FOUR

COUNTERATTACK

Q. My boyfriend says that since most marriages end in divorce, living together first improves the chances for a successful marriage later on. Does it?

A. Your boyfriend is slightly overstating his case. Forty percent of all American marriages end in divorce these days. American couples are experiencing "the seven-year itch" somewhat earlier. The average duration of first marriages which end in divorce is 6½ years.

My research on the alternative of living together produced limited information. I failed to find facts that would substantiate that living together before the first marriage has made a measureable change in the likelihood of its later success.

So read the opening paragraphs of an advice column in a daily newspaper. (Since the column was published, the proportion of divorces has risen to over 50 percent.) That such "advice" could be taken seriously, that such a column could even be published in a family newspaper, is proof of the far-reaching impact of the concerted attack being made against the American home and family.

Consider the question raised: Does living together (in sexual intimacy) before marriage improve the chances that the marriage will succeed? To realize how ludicrous the question is, all you have to do is put it in biblical terminology. In the Bible, remember, what the world calls "living together" is a sin described by the word "fornication." Marriage, as described in the Bible, is God's perfect plan for a man and woman to achieve oneness and to produce and rear children who honor God and contribute strength and wisdom to society.

Rephrased in biblical terms, the question reads like this: Will committing the sin of fornication, specifically condemned by God, help a man and woman fulfill God's sacred design for their lives?

Thus restating the world's question in God's language makes it so obviously absurd that it would be funny were it not so deadly serious. What makes it serious, and gravely so, is that the enemies of the home have so blurred the moral vision of the people that they ask their question in all sincerity. People are so morally insensitive that they actually believe sin offers the key to the "good life." As this relates to our subject, it means they think the sexual sins that destroy interpersonal relationships are the pathway to establishing "meaningful" interpersonal relationships! Deceived into accepting such spiritual nonsense, the masses have become the pawns of the enemies of the home, joining in their merciless effort to destroy marriage and the family.

If boldness wins battles, the defenders of the home have their work cut out for them. Boldness is a conspicuous element in the home wreckers' game plan. In fact, their progress in destroying the home can be measured by the recklessness with which they now attack.

What would have happened to a speaker who came to a quiet middle-class neighborhood twenty or thirty years ago advocating sexual activeness, masturbation, and incest as beneficial for children? The speech would never have been delivered. The townspeople would have ridden the speaker out on a rail as soon as they discovered the topic.

But such speeches are being made across America now—not only openly but somewhat arrogantly. They are advocating that, rather than repress the erotic instincts of the young, society should urge total sexual liberation for children. Not only should kids engage in sexual experimentations, the theory goes, but their parents should encourage them to do so.

Interviewed by a major newspaper, one advocate of no-holds-barred sexual activity for children, Dr. Alayne Yates, Los Angeles psychiatrist and pediatrician, made these observations:

—"I think masturbation needs to be encouraged in children."

—"It's a natural assumption that a person who has positive sexual experiences as a child will enjoy sex later on.

—(But won't encouraging sexual experimentation in the home lead to sibling incest?) "It might. But sibling incest is probably quite common already and relatively normal in families today."

—(The right age for kids to have intercourse) "differs from child to child, of course. I know a 4-year-old boy who had intercourse with a 6-year-old-girl, and neither seemed damaged by it."

—"I'm not aware of any research that demonstrates such a connection (between childhood promiscuity and a detrimental effect on the stability of future marriage).

—"Any kind of early, pleasurable sexual experience tends to augment later sexual adjustment and enthusiasm. And father-daughter incest is frequently pleasurable.

"I must add, however, that the daughter must be young and therefore untouched by the religious and cultural taboos against incest. When a girl is uncoerced by the father and doesn't feel any physical pain, then she probably enjoys it. After all, the vast majority of these cases never come to light."

In other words, there is nothing wrong with this disgusting, emotionally scarring sin. The problem is with the "religious and cultural taboos" against it!

The interviewer asked Dr. Yates: "If kids are taught that sex is good, healthy fun, how can they make the transition to sex that has emotional involvement? In other words what happens to love?"

Dr. Yates' answer: "This transition comes with maturity. Adolescents can't make an emotional commitment until young adulthood. But varied sexual experience in childhood actually facilitates maturation because now the person knows his or her sexual self much better."

Don't get the idea that this is an isolated incident that doesn't prove anything about the lengths to which the enemies of the home are going. If you haven't noticed the free discussion of masturbation, incest, and other sexual sins in your newspaper and on TV, it's because you haven't been paying attention.

These discussions reveal that the enemies of the home know the chief source of opposition to their attack. Like Dr. Yates, most "experts" on the subject blame emotional problems resulting from incest not on the sin but on the Bible and Judeo-Christian morality.

A feature article in my hometown newspaper told of a young girl who was seeing a counselor because she couldn't concentrate on her school work. The counselor said the girl "knew having a sexual relation with her brother was wrong." In eight sessions, the truth came out. "Anna (not her real name) grew up in a highly structured home, strictly sheltered by her parents. At eighteen, she still couldn't date or wear makeup or do things her strict fundamentalist parents felt might lead to sin."

This led the counselor to the only possible conclusion—if you rule out the Holy Spirit working on a sinful conscience: "Any damage in brother-sister incest . . . may come from feelings of guilt and anxiety about people finding out."

Let me emphasize that not all psychiatrists, psychologists, and counselors side with the enemies of the home. Many, perhaps most, still hold that incestuous relationships are emotionally damaging to children. But the advocates of such sexual degradation are growing in number and influence, and their boldness in spreading their decadent ideas is a measure of the success of their offensive against the family.

As Dr. John Parsons pointed out in the material quoted earlier, in God's timetable for emotional development the child is spared from coping with the intricacies of sex until a later period. By forcing the subject on children, and encouraging their parents to do so, the enemies of the home are doing untold damage to the upcoming generation.

But there are more obvious consequences. Venereal disease, for example. Incidents of VD of all types number more than six million annually in America—and half are among teenagers and young adults. The cost to the taxpayers for treating these diseases is more than $80 million a year. If these were any other diseases, people advocating practices that caused such an epidemic to spread would be firmly rebuked.

No so with VD. Those who advocate its spread—indirectly, by encouraging sexual permissiveness—are often treated as the intellectual elite of society!

The effectiveness of the assault on the home can also be seen in attitudes among teenagers and young adults. A New York pyschoanalyst, Dr. Natalie Shainess, summed it up in these words in an article in a medical journal, *Resident and Staff Physician:* "The prevailing attitude is that virginity is something a girl must 'get rid of.'" Dr. Shainess, to her everlasting credit, is one who believes this attitude is destructive to young women.

The assault on the home has stamped itself on the laws that govern us and the court decisions that interpret those laws.

—A 1976 Supreme Court decision allows teenagers to obtain government-supplied contraceptives and abortions without their parents' knowledge.

—The objections of Christians and others to teaching on homosexuality, abortion, contraception, and morals is routinely ignored by schools across the country under laws and court decisions that make the responsible administrators and teachers "untouchable."

—Some states are passing laws lowering the age of sexual consent. In New Jersey, the new law would allow 13-year-olds to consent to sexual intercourse with any partner except a relative, guardian, employer, or teacher. It would permit sexual activity between persons under thirteen as long as neither partner was more than four years older than the other.

Little wonder psychologist Dr. Kenneth Keniston could say, in a 1977 Chicago *Sun Times* issue:

> Parents today remind me of a conductor trying
> to lead an orchestra when all the musicians are

sitting with their backs to him and everyone is
playing from different scores. Most of them are,
I think, relatively helpless and confused. In-
creasingly, they have the feeling that they are
not in control.

How could parents feel they have any control when the state, the national government, the schools, and the rock stars have stolen their children's minds and loyalty?

But parents are not the only ones being left with feelings of confusion and helplessness by the forces working to destroy the family. The values that guided and helped preserve the last generation were not simply an optional lifestyle. They were God-ordained moral tenets. They were based on absolute, eternal truth, not on the whims of a pleasure-addicted society or the political expediency of a handful of self-serving social revolutionaries. Those values can't be exchanged for something else—anything else—without sustaining a loss that affects the very stuff of life. Now young women, lured and pressured into going the way of the "new morality," are experiencing depression, feelings of emptiness and hopelessness, because the "liberation" promised by the feminists has given them no fulfillment. Young men are confused and bitter toward an increase of aggressive, independent, defiant young women.

As God said when he observed man in the Garden of Eden, it is not good for man to be alone. God made man to have a companion. Today's young men need that companion, and they often can't find her among the haughty products of the feminist movement. They may themselves have had "meaningful relationships" with other girls, but they don't want, as their lifetime companion, some other man's leftovers. They are turning to drugs, drink, homosexuality. Many girls, equally frustrated in their new roles, try to fill the void in their lives by becoming pregnant out of wedlock.

The side-effects of the destruction of the God-ordained relationship between men and women reveals itself in a more gruesome statistic, though—the figures that record acts of violence. In the 1970s, violent behavior has mushroomed in the schools, where youngsters spend most of their time outside the home. Assaults on school teachers has increased nearly 80 percent. Rapes and robberies of students and teachers by young people have risen more than 36 percent. Juvenile homicide has gone up 20 percent.

But the most shocking statistic of all shows that, since the Fifties, the suicide rate among teenagers has almost tripled. The most dramatic increase has been among young males fifteen to twenty-four years old. These are the would-be fathers of tomorrow, the heads of households, the spiritual leaders, the community and national leadership of America. Why do so many young people feel that life is not worth living? Dr. Calvin J. Frederick, of the National Institute of Mental Health, explained it this way in a July 1976 interview in *Medical World News:*

> *The most important reason, in my view, is the tendency among young people these days to "do their own thing," to cut themselves off from their parents and society. While this exhibits a certain amount of healthy rebellion and independence, it calls for more strength and wisdom than most young persons possess. Once they cut loose, they suddenly find themselves completely alone,*

unable to manage their new-found freedom
because they have no sense of structure or
belonging. They become frustrated, tense, lonely
and anxious. They decide they can't cope, and
their solution is suicide. The old stability and
structure of the family unit is missing, with
nothing to take its place.

The family, despite the feminist propagandists and the champions of homosexuality and communal living, evidently does contribute something unique and indispensable to personality and character development. What the family contributes is more than just the written, spoken, or unspoken moral and social codes that people live by, as important as those may be. It conveys, in addition, a sense of "structure or belonging." That's a vague and hard-to-define ingredient. But it gives a young person a confidence about having come from somewhere and about the desirability of going somewhere in the future. It carries with it a feeling of responsibility, a sense of being part of a continuum, a link in a chain that should not be broken.

This something that the family imparts is invaluable in helping young people understand their identity and purpose for life. When the family is prevented from instilling this all-important contribution—or its work is nullified by the brainwashing of the enemy—the young perish and, evenually, society crumbles.

Several times I have alluded to collectivism, socialism, or totalitarianism in discussing the ideas and actions of the enemies of the home. No treatment of this subject would be complete, however, without a specific word about this aspect of the issue.

Much of the ideology that serves as a philosophical

base for the attack on the family, and much of the rhetoric used by the home wreckers, flows directly from Marx-Leninism. Many of the prime movers in the attack are persons long known for their devotion to the cause of replacing free enterprise in America by means of a (hopefully) bloodless socialist revolution.

The pamphleteers of the various anti-family groups often betray their dedication to goals that lie beyond the boundaries of their stated cause.

For example, Feminist Kate Millet wrote in *Sexual Politics* (Doubleday, 1970):

> *In America one may expect the new women's movement to ally itself on an equal basis with blacks and students in a growing radical coalition. It is also possible that women now represent a very crucial element capable of swinging the national mood, poised at this moment between the alternatives of progress or political repression, toward meaningful change. As the largest alienated element in our society—and because of their numbers, passion, and length of oppression, its largest revolutionary base—women might come to play a leadership part in social revolution, quite unknown before in history. The changes in fundamental values such a coalition of expropriated groups—blacks, youth, women, the poor—would seek are especially pertinent to realizing not only sexual revolution but a gathering impetus toward freedom from rank or prescriptive role, sexual or otherwise.*

In other words, a comaraderie exists between feminism and other movements striving to disrupt American social and political structures.

Some groups are more open in revealing the real

thrust of their ideology. In the writings of the notoriously Marx-Leninist Students for Democratic Society, this statement appeared:

> The struggle for equality of women is a revolutionary task—that is, one which cannot be completed under the present system of private property and the exploitation of the majority of people by a social class which is defined by its ownership of the means of producing wealth . . . The fight for women's liberation is a concretization of the struggle for the liberation of all people from oppression. It doesn't stand apart from the fight against capitalism in our society, but rather is an integral part of that fight.

Feminism's most disarming tactic is to claim that "equal pay for equal work" is really what the movement is all about.

But its own literature belies that posture. Jo Freeman, author of *The Politics of Women's Liberation*, (published in 1975 by McKay Publishers) says:

> Most feminists . . . share a set of common ideas and symbols which provide for a basic unity . . . Unlike many sectarian leftist groups, (in women's lib) different activities are seen more as a division of labor than as a means of divisiveness.

And in her book *New Feminist Movement* (Russell Sage Foundation, 1974), sociologist Maren Carden observes:

> Whether they accept the less radical or the more radical interpretation of the ideology, Women's Liberation participants become committed to that ideology in the same way. They exchange

127

accounts of personal experiences, identify shared problems, and interpret these problems in terms of the movement's ideology. Having examined all aspects of their lives from this new perspective, they eventually reconceptualize their thinking and accept that perspective as the correct way to interpret women's experience.

Many well-meaning women see injustices in the marketplace and support the feminists' push for "equal pay for equal work." If they become actively involved in the movement, however, they are exposed to the basically Marxist ideology that permeates it. Many—some perhaps without even realizing what is happening—begin to accept the Marxist perspective. Soon they are completely indoctrinated. They view not only the specific problems of women in the marketplace but all issues and values from the perspective of Marxist philosophy.

Marxism's strategy has always been to exploit the problems of free society (the "contradictions," Marx called them) as weapons to destroy freedom. Thus every purported effort to solve a problem must be examined for the Marxist strings that may be attached. A man who became keenly aware of this—Casper W. Weinberger—made these pertinent remarks in a speech he delivered on retiring as secretary of Health, Education, and Welfare in 1975:

Our country was built by people of energy, daring, and ingenuity—the Edisons, the Wright Brothers, the Helen Kellers, the Fultons, the Carnegies, the great musicians and artists, and countless others brimming with dreams and filled with the courage to reach out and realize those dreams whatever the odds.

Their kind of daring was nurtured in a social climate that rewarded risk-takers and practical visionaries. If we now proceed mindlessly to change that climate to one favoring a faceless gray egalitarianism, we will have lost all that has made America great and enabled us to help so much of the world.

The real social agenda of America, still unfinished, is to discover and reward excellence wherever we find it—under a black skin, a white skin, in a female or male, in a Catholic, a Jew, a Protestant, or an agnostic. That is the real purpose of equal opportunity.

If we fail to see this as our real agenda, we risk delivering our destinies over to the cold and lifeless grip of a distant egalitarian government whose sole purpose is to ensure an equally mediocre existence for everyone, achieved at the cost of personal liberty.

The coalition of feminist, humanist, socialist, gay liberationist, and anti-family elements in America today seems bent on delivering America into the "cold and lifeless grip" of just such an egalitarian dictatorship.

Everyone who loves freedom and decency should know this, and the knowledge should spur us to act— immediately and with every resource at our command— to preserve our heritage of liberty.

SUGGESTED STRATEGIES

When Christians awaken to the all-out assault being staged against everything they cherish, many feel a sense of helplessness. "What can I do?" they ask. "I'm just one person."

The situation is not hopeless. The battle is not lost. The nation is made up of "one persons." The attempt to destroy the family and America's freedoms is being made by "one persons" who have joined themselves with other "one persons" to get things done their way.

You, as just one person, together with your friends and others who believe as you do, can be just as effective if you are willing to commit yourself to a course of action.

Christians can be far more effective than the atheistic forces, because they have the power of intercessory prayer at their disposal.

I believe the only real hope for the family and for America as a free nation is intervention by God himself to preserve the structures he has ordained. But I do not believe God will step in until those who call themselves his people rise up, identify themselves, and take a firm stand for what they know to be right and godly.

Second Chronicles 7:14 is a familiar verse to most church-going Christians: "If my people, which are called by my name, shall humble themselves, and pray, and seek my face, and turn from their wicked ways; then will I hear from heaven and will forgive their sin, and will heal their land."

At no time has it been more urgent for American Christians to heed that verse. Before God will intervene to "heal their land," Christians must humble themselves. Too many of us have been depending on America's riches, its nuclear-tipped missiles, its mighty traditions, and the "basic goodness" of its people. We must recognize that none of these is sufficient, that we must depend solely on God and his wisdom and power. We must call on him to intervene, not just in the affairs of our country but in our own lives, to make us what he wants us to be. We must seek his face. We must seek holiness, because he is a holy God and we are to be holy as he is holy (1 Peter 1:16). We must repent—"turn from . . . wicked ways." Righteousness, and righteousness alone, exalteth a nation, and sin is a reproach to any people (Proverbs 14:34).

Christians must also remember the redemptive, missionary purpose God purchased us and placed us in the world to fulfill. God did not send his Son to die for us to save the American free enterprise system, American political ideals, or even the American family, precious as those things are. He has sent us into the world for the same purpose as he sent Christ (John 20:21). Many Scriptures state that purpose but none more succinctly than John 3:17: "For God sent not his Son into the world to condemn the world; but that the world through him might be saved."

The verse says "the world"—not just us as individuals, our homes, our families, our comfortable lifestyles, and not just America—the entire world. To stir God's interest in America to the point that he will intervene to save her, Christians must dedicate themselves and call their fellow countrymen to a commitment to preach the gospel to all nations. When enough people have turned to God and made this commitment to make this country a base camp for evangelizing the world, I believe God will move miraculously to save America.

Your first step in combating the heathen forces attacking the home and the country, then, should be to make your own total commitment to be used as an instrument of God in winning the world to Christ.

The next step should be to help call your church, your denomination, your community, and the entire country to a similar commitment. God can be trusted to keep his promises. If his people will identify with him and set themselves aside to be used in the fulfillment of his purpose, he will "heal their land."

Even as you attend to these spiritual responsibilities, however, you should start asserting yourself as a Christian citizen in a free country—while you are still free to do so.

The basic formula for active Christian citizenship is: Be inspired, be informed, be involved.

To be inspired simply means to pray for God's wisdom and power in everything you set out to do. Christ in you is the hope of glory (Colossians 1:27). We don't dare tackle the complex issues and vicious forces of the political arena without Christ guiding and strengthening us.

You must also be informed. You must know who the enemy is, his strategy, and the objectives he is pursuing. That means you should read everything you can find about humanism, feminism and the various "liberation" movements, and what they are doing in every field. You should familiarize yourself with groups opposing these forces, read their printed materials, attend some of their meetings, talk to their members, and hear their speakers. Above all, you should be firmly grounded in the doctrines of your own faith and the basis for your moral values. And you should strive to become an expert in the American political system and all its workings. The enemy does his homework. He know what makes the system tick.

This sounds like work, and it is. But you will find it stimulating and rewarding.

Just one word of caution: Call on God's powers of discernment in evaluating all information, from whatever source. As always, there are today many wolves in sheep's clothing. Some groups that claim to defend American traditions or Christian values actually foment hatred, fear, and suspicion. The primary insurance against being deceived by such individuals and groups is to remember that they cannot be of God because fear, hatred, and suspicion are not godly characteristics.

What can one person do? Remember: Jesus Christ is one Person!

CHILDREN FIRST

Defenders of the family should choose a strategy that deals with the most serious threat first—the attack directed against the home through our children. The public schools are the major arena for this aspect of the conflict.

Parents and all concerned citizens should act quickly, vigorously, and persistently to expose and block humanist-feminist-socialist inroads into school curricula and teaching approaches. These include textbooks and other teaching materials that promote a genderless society and collectivism, as well as sex-education courses that undermine traditional values pertaining to marriage, the family, and sexual morality.

The pro-family counterattack in the schools also should draw a bead on more subtle humanist tactics. Any program bearing a "mental health" label, for example, could well be a humanist wolf in sheep's clothing. Since the end of World War II, humanist militants have been pursuing their goals behind a mental health front. Their definition of mental health is far broader than the generally accepted one, however. It connotes a "state of complete physical, mental, and social well-being, and not merely the absence of disease or infirmity." If freed from impairments to such mental health, the humanists assert, mankind could eliminate war, crime, and other social blights, along with what are commonly termed mental illnesses. Improving the mental health of children, then, can include such objectives as ridding their formative minds of "religious myths" and "moral taboos" instilled by "fundamentalist" parents and churches.

Instruments used in the mental cleansing of school children include an endless assortment of questionnaires and pamphlets kept flowing into the schools. The pamphlets are sprinkled with humanist psychiatric and psychological propaganda pertaining to the basic concepts of humanity.

Most schools conduct valid IQ or aptitude tests to help determine students' abilities and direct them into the fields in which they are best qualified to succeed. These are not the tests defenders of the family should fight. Enemies of the family often oppose these tests because their results don't always support their ideological assumptions.

Defenders of the family should oppose the so-called psychological testing that is used to influence children's thoughts and gather information about their parents and their home environment. Questions on tests of this type are phrased to suggest to students certain attitudes and conclusions. Parents should warn their children to refuse to take tests containing references to religion, home, life, sex attitudes, political exposure, and other personal matters. All citizens interested in preserving the traditional family should protest the use of such tests to school boards, local school administrators, and state and national representatives in government.

To protect their children from the humanist attack

in the schools, parents should practice these simple precautions:

—Examine the textbooks and other printed materials the child is assigned to read. Watch for subtle promotion of immoral conduct or anti-family, anti-American content.

—Encourage the child to refuse to discuss personal feelings or family life at school, and assure him that his refusal is not a symptom of mental problems.

—Warn the child to be on guard against role playing and other group "games" that force him to deal with hypothetical situations through questions that ask, "What would you do if . . . ?" These activities have been used by the humanists to scramble youngsters' attitudes toward moral values, leaving them vulnerable to the substitution of humanist values. When the questions deal with such subjects as suicide and mercy killing they can cause emotional trauma.

—Arrange to view films shown the child at school. If such films contain objectionable material, a protest should be made to the principal. If that official fails to remove the film, the matter should be taken to the school board.

—Brief the child on humanism, its techniques and strategies, and warn him to be alert for it. Humanism has been declared a religion by the U. S. Supreme Court. The forced teaching of humanism in the public schools is a violation of the U. S. Constitution. Both parent and child have a right to resist compulsory exposure to humanist propaganda as part of a prescribed curriculum.

—Urge and assist other parents and concerned citizens to get involved in the counterattack against humanism in the schools. They can act as individuals, but group activity usually gives better results. It facilitates the needed exchange of information and coordination of actions. But what is more important, it provides the strength in numbers that is often necessary to effect changes in school policies.

Sports has coined the phrase, "Hang tough." And defenders of the family must be prepared to do just that in their struggle to protect their children in the schools. The enemy will do everything possible to intimidate those who take a stand, to make them appear ignorant, out of date, or fanatical. In so doing, they will often have the cooperation, either unwitting or deliberate, of the secular press. Here, for example, are excerpts from a report in my hometown paper on a public hearing at which parents cited the threat of humanism in the schools:

> A special committee got an earful Wednesday on how to cure public education's ills—primarily by cutting away all but the essential subjects.
>
> During a public hearing by the Governor's Advisory Committee on Education in Fort Worth..., parents testified overwhelmingly against experimental courses that deal with nontraditional values.
>
> Railing against the evils of "humanism," many parents said public schools should drop "values education" and get back to teaching reading, writing, and arithmetic.
>
> Calling techniques used in courses such as drug and sex education and values clarification "humanistic and atheistic," more than a dozen parents urged public schools not to clutter their curricula with "social change" courses.
>
> "Parents do not believe that public schools exist for the sole purpose of social change," one witness told the committee. "Please stop the

experimentation with the minds of our children. Let's get rid of the facilitators and get some teachers in the classroom.

In emotional appeals to turn the clock back about 20 years, the speakers said that public schools are being used "in massive attempt to destroy our country" by teaching the principles of "humanism."

While condemning "values education," however, most of the parents indicated they would like public schools to support traditional values such as God, the United States, and the work ethic.

About 60 persons, almost exclusively white and female, testified before nine committee members . . .

The reporter, who was not identified by a by-line, may not have been a trained humanist propagandist. But if he or she had been, the report could not have been more subtly slanted to destroy the credibility of the concerned parents' testimony.

Humanistic and humanism appear in quotation marks throughout, as though these are not valid terms identifying a real movement but mere figments of the imaginations of paranoid minds. It would make just as much sense to put communism in quotes.

The testimony against humanism is described as "railing," the pleas for a stop to the brainwashing as "emotional appeals." These are derogatory terms suggesting that the parents' case is an irrational unleashing of pentup emotions, rather than a reasoned argument with a firm basis in fact.

The slur implied in the reference to turning the clock back is obvious. This says that those opposing the indoctrination of our children in the atheistic and immoral philosophies of secular humanism are backward obstructions to progress.

The report also insinuates that the defenders of the home are just another special interest group trying to have its way. They want the kind of "values education" now being taught removed so they can substitute their own, it suggests. It does not reflect the fact that the values supported by the parents are not their private beliefs but the truths on which the country, its laws, and its culture were founded and have flourished.

Those who take a public stand for the family and the values it rests upon must expect this kind of tacit ridicule. But we must not be deterred from waging our battle. God's will is that we speak the truth whether it is accepted or not, that we stand for righteousness whatever the consequences. If we are faithful to do so, he promises to heal our land.

WHAT ONE PERSON CAN DO

One group organized for the defense of the family, Pro-Family Forum, urges friends of the family to support these basic positions in addition to opposing humanism in the schools:

—The biblical principle of man's role as head of his home, leader, and provider.

—The traditional role of motherhood.

—Protection of parents' authority to train their children.

—The rights of all, including youth, to have access to the truth about humanism.

—The removal of TV programming detrimental to public morals.

—The preservation of human life from conception to natural death.

For anyone determined to do battle against the enemies of the family, that would be a sound platform. Any doctrine, movement, or activity that conflicts with those principles should be vehemently counter-attacked, because it militates against the family and basic American values.

How do you counterattack? The same group lists a number of actions that any concerned individual can easily take, including:

—Arrange for speakers for the pro-family positions to address your church, club, or other group.

—Display posters and distribute printed materials calling attention to the threat to the family and informing people on what to do.

—Provide counseling for youth confused by the humanist misinformation on drugs, abortion, sex, and suicide.

—Alert your church, individuals, and other groups to write or call stations about upcoming objectionable TV programming.

—Participate in the nationwide boycott of products of manufacturers sponsoring such programming.

—Write letters to the editors of newspapers and magazines supporting the pro-family side of issues in the news.

—Contribute financially to groups that fight for the family and publish and distribute materials support-ive of the family.

—Volunteer to help a pro-family group prepare and mail printed materials and to build attendance at its meetings.

—Become an active member of a group dedicated to

defending and promoting the family.

The key is to be informed and be alert to issues that call for immediate action on the part of family defenders.

The feminist-humanist push for ratification of the Equal Rights Amendment, for example, provides an almost continuous demand for response from friends of the family.

When the President or his wife or any other member of the administration beats the drums for ratification, that is cause for action. It is a misappropriation of public funds for these people to use our tax money to lobby for one side of an issue that is not under jurisdiction of the executive branch in the first place.

When almost every major magazine in the country publishes pro-ERA articles in a single month with no presentation of the opposing view, as happened in November 1979, that is a cause for action. Such a propaganda barrage could hardly be a coincidence. It was planned by the enemies of the home and carried out with the complicity of the editors. Every such effort to misguide the people and exploit a misinformed public should be exposed through letters to magazines, newspapers, and government figures and countered by a storm of protest.

When ERA proponents vow to use every means, both fair and foul, to get their way—as when Margo St. James, president of COYOTE boasted she would take prostitutes into unratified states and win ratification by exposing their clients in the state legislatures—that is a cause for action. Blackmail or any illegal or loathsome tactic of the enemy should be identified and denounced.

In addition to writing letters to the editor and

contacting congressmen, family defenders should be alert for opportunities to attend rallies and demonstrations in support of their cause. Enemies of the home and of biblical values have consistently taken to the streets to make their cause visible and win clout through media exposure. Because of the anti-family bias of much of the media, friends of the home cannot expect coverage matching that given the radical elements, but we must not be discouraged.

The March for Life demonstration in Washington, D.C., which I addressed from the steps of the Capitol, got media coverage. The TV people may not have been sympathetic to this protest against abortion-on-demand, but they could hardly ignore a crowd of 80,000 sign-bearing demonstrators winding through the streets of the capital.

Ignorance is no excuse for refusing to get involved in the fight to save the family. Seminars are held in major cities across the country several times a year by various pro-family groups. Attendance fees are nominal. Anyone interested enough in saving the family to get informed and involved can find ample opportunity to do so. Those who are not able to attend a seminar can write to the pro-family groups and get on their mailing lists for newsletters and publications.

Conferences and public hearings at every level of government give opportunity for the pro-family side to be heard where it counts most. Defenders of the family should watch for notices of such events and plan to attend or send others.

In some cases—the 1980 White House Conference on Families, for instance—states or communities are asked to send delegations selected by a specific process. Friends of the family should make certain that delegations from their state or community contain a strong proportion of persons representing the pro-family side of the issue involved.

Family defenders should watch with wholesome suspicion every action and tendency of every branch of government and respond with appropriate opposition to every sign of anti-family bias.

One area demanding the utmost vigilance is the judiciary. The federal courts have done more than perhaps either of the other two branches of government to destroy the traditional family and undermine the values that made America the greatest nation in the history of the world. Two U. S. Supreme Court decisions serve to illustrate the point.

The first, handed down in 1962, banished voluntary prayer from the public schools. The ruling was based on the First Amendment prohibition of an establishment of religion. That is ironic, because the decision had the effect of violating that very clause. By banning voluntary prayer and reading of sacred literature of other religions, particularly Christianity, but not the teachings of secular humanism, the court in effect established secular humanism as the state religion in the schools. Both the literature presenting humanist dogma and the instruction of students in these teachings are funded by the state.

The decision violated the First Amendment in an even more blatant way, however. For it is, on its very face, a restriction of the free exercise of religion, which the amendment clearly guarantees.

Another Supreme Court decision, the 1973 ruling upholding the right of women to have abortions up to three months of pregnancy, may be an even more dangerous threat to the family and American values. In that decision, the court established the authority of government to determine who shall be regarded as a "person" in the eyes of the law and, therefore, who shall be entitled to the rights and privileges protected by the Constitution. In effect, this means the government has arrogated to itself the power to decide who has the right to live. This despite the ringing endorsement given the sanctity of life in our Declaration of Independence, which holds that God has extended to all the right to "life, liberty, and the pursuit of happiness"!

Many people feel a sense of helplessness in opposing the anti-family tendencies shown by the courts, but there are things that can be done.

First, though federal judges and Supreme Court justices are appointed for life and so are not subject to being voted out of office, they are not impervious to public opinion. In politics there is a saying, "Judges read the newspaper, too." They can be influenced by trends in public attitudes. In fact, their anti-family decisions are largely the result of the influence of the humanists and other foes of the family. To change the direction of the courts, then, the one priority of the pro-family movement should be to sway as much public opinion as possible to the support of the family.

Second, pro-family citizens should speak up in protest of court decisions with anti-family impact. It is for certain that enemies of the family will publicly praise rulings favoring their view.

In January 1980 U. S. District Judge John F. Dooling of Brooklyn, N.Y., held unconstitutional the Hyde Amendment, a federal law drastically reducing the use of public funds to pay for abortions. The law was enacted at the behest of pro-family citizens trying to minimize the impact of the 1973 abortion ruling.

Immediately, the media cranked up a campaign to

applaud the decision. Stories appeared in which pro-abortion figures hailed the ruling as a victory for the poor. Actually, the amendment's greatest impact was to reduce federally-funded abortions from 250,000 to 13,000 annually, thus preventing the murder of countless of the innocent unborn.

Since the decision has been appealed to the Supreme Court, what the judges hear from the populace could weigh heavily in the outcome. They will certainly hear the anti-family view. It is the responsibility of every Christian and every decent citizen to see that they hear the pro-family side, too. The justices must know that a large and growing majority of the American people regard life as a priceless gift of God and the government's responsibility is one of protecting and preserving it, not destroying it. The jurists might be reminded that, had they been denied the right to live, others would be occupying their places on the bench.

Another approach to changing the humanistic trend in court decisions is to influence judgeship appointments. Often, the motive behind these appointments is the need to pay a political debt or garner political support, rather than preserving priceless values. For example, in 1979, President Carter appointed Ruth Bader Ginsburg to the U. S. Circuit Court of Appeals, the country's second most important court. Judge Ginsburg has been a vocal advocate of feminism and the ERA. Some Washington columnists reported that she had been promised an appointment later to the U. S. Supreme Court.

Many pro-family groups and individuals protested the appointment vociferously and urged their senators to vote against approval. Every family-loving American should have joined in demanding that this person not be placed in a position to rule on the future of the home and the biblical foundations of U. S. society.

This is but one of thousands of appointments the President is authorized to make. Defenders of the family should keep an eye on them all, especially the judiciary appointments, and urge their senators to vote against approval of those with anti-family records.

The executive branch of government also deserves close attention. Under its wing huddles what some have come to call a "fourth branch" of government—one not established by the Constitution and not accountable to the voters. The reference is to the sprawling federal bureaucy, the maze of departments, agencies, and commissions that have sprung up to implement federal legislation.

In an organization—sometimes it looks more like a disorganization—as massive as this, bureaucracy, confusion, and conflict often reign. Not infrequently, the effect of an entire policy or activity depends on the mind-set of one or a handful of low-echelon functionaries.

Stated briefly, the duty of the government bureaucracy is to formulate the directives and regulations necessary to put into effect the laws and programs passed by Congress and signed by the President. Sometimes when the bureaucracy has finished "promulgating" and "implementing," however, the result is something neither Congress nor the President intended.

Friends of the family must be diligent in watching for governmental regulations and operations that militate against the family. When these activities violate the intent of Congress, a word to a congressman can start a movement in the legislative branch to pressure the offending agency to change its policy. Often, however, the flaw is in the law: what Congress intended simply was not an effective approach to the problem, as seen from the perspective of the family.

For that reason, family supporters should take special interest in the legislative branch. So many bills are introduced that few receive the public airing they deserve before being either enacted or killed. Bills that do get considerable exposure are often either so complicated, or so poorly discussed in the press, that ordinary citizens find it hard to determine all of their ramifications.

A number of Christian and pro-family organizations have the staff and resources to monitor congressional action on matters affecting the family. Concerned persons should avail themselves of information disseminated by these groups. To be well informed, one would be wise to balance the output of the mass media with communications from a variety of sources. Relying on a single source can result in loss of perspective and credibility.

At this writing, many laws and legislative actions pending congressional action would affect the family for good or bad. Some of those that are a part of the humanist attack on the family are:

—A Revision of the U. S. Criminal Code. Along with some needed changes in U. S. criminal law, the latest version of the proposed updating of the criminal code includes protection for pornographers and other evildoers.

—The Domestic Violence Act. Though gaining impetus from the highly publicized incidence of child abuse and wife beating, this noble-sounding proposal is a legislative Trojan Horse bearing precepts that would be disastrous to the traditional family. It would authorize government invasion of the home and interference in Bible-based parental discipline.

—Test-Tube Babies. A bill legalizing certain "genetic engineering" and extrauterine reproduction techniques would allow the government to "play God" by choosing who could be parents and who could be born.

—Parental Kidnapping. Under this proposed law, parents who attempted to get their children back after having them removed from the home for legal reasons could be charged with kidnapping.

Federal legislative proposals that would benefit the family include:

—The Child Health Assurance Plan as passed by the House of Representatives in December 1979. In this form, the bill contained four amendments attached by pro-family members of Congress. A companion bill introduced in the Senate at this writing had not been similarly amended and was dangerous as it stood.

—The Voluntary School Prayer Amendment. Authored by Sen. Jesse Helms (R-N.C.) this amendment to the U. S. Constitution would remove the prayer question from federal court jurisdiction and, in effect, restore the right of voluntary prayer and Bible reading to public schools. The amendment passed the Senate as a rider attached to a piece of judicial legislation. In the House, it stuck in the House Judiciary Committee. At this writing, pro-family forces are striving to get the required 218 members of Congress to sign a discharge petition that would dislodge the measure from the committee and let its fate be decided by a vote of the full House.

—The Family Protection Act. As introduced by Sen. Paul Laxalt (R.-Nev.), this bill contained thirty-eight provisions designed to help traditional families survive the pressure of industrialized society and the humanist machinations of government.

Though the legislation is lengthy, the following summary of the thirty-eight concepts embodied in the bill, published by *Conservation Digest,* offers a concise view of the sweeping scope of action that would be necessary to save the family:

Title I. Education

1. Federal education money is denied states that don't allow prayer in public buildings.

2. Federal money is denied states that don't require parental consent for student enrollment in public school courses about religion.

3. Federal money is denied schools that try to exclude parents from visiting public school classrooms or functions.

4. Federal money is denied schools that require public school teachers to belong to a union.

5. Federal money is denied states that don't permit parental and community review of textbooks prior to their use in public schools.

6. Federal money is denied values clarification or behavior modification courses.

7. Federal money may not buy textbooks or other educational materials that belittle the traditional role of women in society.

8. States are insured the right to determine teacher qualifications, free from the influence of federal regulations.

9. States are insured the exclusive authority to regulate attendance at public schools.

10. Local schools are given back the authority over sex-intermingling in sports and other school activities.

11. Private schools are exempted from National Labor Relations Board jurisdiction.

12. A Family Savings for Education Plan is established: Parents may deposit up to $2,500, tax-exempt,

per year, to save for their children's education.

13. Most titles of the Elementary and Secondary Education Act are repealed and replaced with block grants of money to states to use for education as they deem necessary.

14. If schools require a parenthood course, parents may arrange for their children to be taught the course by a minister or church on a release-time basis.

15. Parent-run schools are granted tax exemption if they fulfill certain requirements, and are granted accreditation for all purposes of federal education law.

16. Federal courts are denied jurisdiction over the issue of voluntary prayer in public buildings and the issue of state requirements for teacher selection and promotion.

Title II. Welfare

17. A tax credit of $250 is allowed a household which includes a dependent person age 65 or over (Multigenerational Household Incentive).

18. A tax exemption of $1,000 is allowed a household which includes a dependent person age 65 or over.

19. College students may not receive food stamps.

20. A corporation may deduct from taxes its contribution to a joint employee-employer day care facility.

21. The pre-1973 Defense Department requirement that servicemen separated from their families send their dependents an allowance is reinstated.

Title III. First Amendment Guarantees

22. Rights of Religious Institutions. Federal agencies may not regulate religious activities such as church schools, religious homes, and other ministries.

23. Rights of Families. Parental rights over the

religious and moral upbringing of their children are reinforced.

Title IV. Taxation

24. Contributions by an employed person to a savings account for his nonworking spouse are tax deductible, up to $1,500 per year.

25. The current "marriage tax," which penalizes married couples with two incomes, is eliminated.

26. Expenses incurred in connection with charitable, civil, political, or religious volunteer work are given the child care credit.

27. Married couples filing jointly are granted an additional $1,000 tax exemption for the year in which a child is either born or adopted. The exemption increases to $3,000 if the child is adopted and either handicapped, over the age of three, or biracial.

28. Contributions to an IRA-type retirement account for the taxpayer's parents are deductible, up to $1,500 per year for each parent.

Title V. Domestic Relations

29. Child Abuse. Federal attempts to change state statutes on child abuse are forbidden. Spankings are specifically stated as not constituting abuse. Federal funds for operation of a child abuse program without specific authorization from the state legislature are prohibited.

30. Spouse Abuse. State statutes regarding family relationships are protected from federal interference. Private associations to care for domestic violence victims are encouraged.

31. State statutes regarding juvenile delinquency are protected from federal interference. Tax-exempt status is granted to private associations working on the problem, providing no federal funds are received.

32. Parents must be informed when an unmarried

minor receives contraceptive appliances or abortion-related services from a federally supported organization.

33. Legal Services Corporation money may not be used in litigation seeking to compel abortions, assistance, or compliance with abortion, or funding for abortions.

34. Legal Services money may not be used for school desegregation litigation.

35. Legal Services funds may not be used for divorce litigation.

36. Legal Services funds may not be used for homosexual rights litigation.

37. Federal money is denied any organization that presents homosexuality as an acceptable alternative lifestyle.

38. Discrimination against declared homosexuals may not be considered an "unlawful employment practice."

While the busy tentacles of the federal government demand our attention, they cannot be allowed to divert our gaze entirely from what state and local government are doing. Many humanist strategies—the ERA, to name one prominent example—depend ultimately on the cooperation of state legislatures. Many anti-family programs of the federal government call for state and/or local participation. Other humanist objectives—such as the "New Generation" child health plan and federally funded child-care network—are now being sought from state to state, having run into problems at the federal level.

Locally, city councils are responsible for ordinances that directly affect the life-style of the community. Within their area of responsibility are laws pertaining to pornography, prostitution, obscenity, and other areas related to the security of the family. Pro-family citizens should urge their city fathers constantly to enact good, enforceable laws on these issues.

The mere enactment of ordinances is not enough to assure results, unfortunately. Often, laws are passed but never enforced by the police. Prosecutors also have been known to be lax in filing charges against arrested offenders and bringing them to trial.

To be sure that the family is being protected in their communities, defenders of the family must exert pressure on their law-enforcement agencies to enforce pro-family ordinances and prosecute all offenders.

Humanism has not confined its infiltration to the realms of government and the schools. To a surprising degree, it has also made significant inroads into private industry. Traces of humanist influence surface constantly in corporate giving policies and in the grant decisions of private foundations. The literature of the corporations and foundations tells its own story. The Exxon Corporation's booklet, *Dimensions '78,* for example, listed these contributions:

American Civil Liberties Union (ACLU)	$20,000
Aspen Institute for Humanistic Studies	$25,000
Feminist Press	$ 5,000
MS Foundation for Women	$10,000
Population Research Center	$20,000

The booklet says these gifts are made in the "public interest." The "public" whose interests they support seems a very narrow one, however. While the humanists are well represented on the list of recipients, not one gift went to an organization dedicated to preserving the traditional or biblical family.

Friends of the family should watch corporation and foundation reports for such anti-family policies. Such reports are available in libraries and through pro-family groups that monitor industry publications.

Christians and other concerned citizens have at their disposal a most effective weapon for defending the family and Bible-based ethics and morality. In addition to being perhaps the most powerful weapon available, it is one of the least expensive. It is also so simple that almost anyone past third grade can learn to use it with a minimum of time and effort.

What is this "ultimate weapon"? It is called a letter.

Many of the evils that have descended on the American marketplace, the schools, and the family could have been forstalled if concerned people had bothered to write to the leaders responsible for decisions in the affected areas.

Why don't more people write? In most cases, because of the common ailment known as procrastination. We say, "I am going to write and let So-And-So know what I think about that." But pen and paper may not be handy at the moment, and we never get around to composing the letter.

For those who seriously want to start getting America back onto its biblical foundations, I recommend forming the habit of having a pen and notepad near at all times. Carry them in your purse or coatpocket as you go about your daily routine. Have them on your coffee table as you watch TV. And use them. When something you observe prompts you to write, make some quick notes of your impressions. Get the name of the person or institution you want to write to. If you don't have the address, you can usually get it later with a phone call.

Then, at the earliest possible moment, before your notes get "cold," write that letter and mail it. Correct grammar and a crisp writing style are nice to have, but they are by no means essential to writing a letter that will produce results. People in positions of responsibility *do* read and take heed of mail from their constituents. When Christians have written in numbers to leaders, they have been able to get things done. Before there can be many letters, though, there must be one. If you don't write yours, there might be none.

Other Christians fail to write because they do not know how to compose a proper letter. While skillful composition is not of supreme importance, it can be learned with little effort. In fact, counselor-Bible teacher Bill Gothard has designed a thirteen-point approach which, if followed, should result in an effective letter to anyone in a leadership position. His suggestions:

1. Identify yourself. You increase your credibility by describing yourself as a constituent, campaign contributor, precinct worker, an active citizen (member of civic group, religious organization, etc.).

2. Be friendly. "Letters from thoughtful friends or undecided voters have more influence than letters from implacable enemies," Gothard says. A railing letter is likely to be dismissed as the emotional outburst of a crackpot. Besides, if you are a Christian, it is important for you to be a witness.

3. Give praise. You should write when you are pleased as well as when you are disgruntled. However, if you have neglected to write when you were pleased, start your letter of complaint with generous recognition of things the person or institution has done that you did like.

4. Stick to one subject. Persons in leadership are very busy—or should be. They rarely have time to read long letters fully and carefully. It is far better to

write often on separate issues and keep each letter short.

5. Be neat and brief. Type if you can. If not, write or print neatly and clearly, leaving plenty of margin and space between lines to make your letter easy to read. "Write a short opening, two or three paragraphs . . . and a short closing," Gothard says. Try not to go over one page.

6. Address properly. Use "The honorable" before the title of a representative, senator, or other official. Then be sure to get the title right. It is usually possible to get correct addresses of public officials from your local newspaper. Most political action groups have directories of persons in government.

7. Know your subject. Know how a proposal or government action (or TV program or magazine article) violates biblical principles or harms the family. Identify legislation by a bill number or the name by which it is commonly known, such as "Domestic Violence Act." Don't just be negative. Suggest other approaches to the problem at issue.

8. Be specific. Avoid generalities such as "This is humanistic." Tell why its being humanistic makes it undesirable. Ask the leader if he will take the action you request regarding the matter. Ask him, if he will not, please to write you and explain his position.

9. Add weight. If you are making a report to your church or other group on the subject, say so. Use newspaper clippings or quotes from knowledgeable people to support your argument. Gothard suggests writing a "Letter to the Editor" of your local paper and mailing a copy of it with your letter to let the leader know you are influencing others.

10. No "form letters." Mass-produced letters that

are only signed and mailed have little influence. They suggest that you don't take the trouble to think for yourself. A poorly written letter of your own is better than a "slick" piece of writing done by someone else for you. Never name another person or group as the source of your thoughts.

11. If you want a reply, ask for it. "It never hurts to try to get a commitment (from the leader you are writing to)," Gothard says.

12. Write often. Don't think a single letter is going to change the world. Two or three letters a month to the same leader are not too many, if you have that many valid subjects to write about.

13. Pray first. Gothard says: "Pray for the one to whom you are writing. Ask God to bind and rebuke Satan for any deception which would cause a rejection of God's principles. Fervent prayer avails much."

THE LAST TRUMPET

Interviewed on his ninetieth birthday in 1975, philosopher-historian Will Durant mourned the decline of marriage and the family. He said:

> *That is unfortunate, because they are two marvelous forms of order that can be pillars of strength in the flux of modern life. If you get rid of the state, the family can maintain order. But get rid of the family and you have nothing.*

Marriage and the family have not disappeared entirely, but they exist in a weakened state, and the destructive impact of this development on society is frighteningly evident. With five out of nine marriages ending in divorce, discipline is vanishing not only from the home and school but from the nation.

Over one million young people run away from home each year. Drug and alcohol abuse have reached epidemic proportions. An estimated 43 million Americans, including more than 75 percent of our high school students, have experimented with marijuana. Some 10 million have tried cocaine. The number of heroin addicts has increased tenfold in the last two decades. Of the 10 million alcoholics in America, nearly a million and a half are teenagers.

In the twenty years from 1960 to 1980, violent crimes have risen from 100 to 200 percent in most categories. In 1979, over 1,200,000 abortions were recorded.

More sickening than these statistics, however, is the unmeasured damage caused by the crippling of the institutions of marriage and the family: The happiness never experienced. The fulfillment never known. The love never expressed, or felt. The deep psychological wounds inflicted on innocent children by the rejection of confused parents and the indoctrination of an educational system and a society awash with atheistic humanism.

Popular writings abound with evidence of how pervasive and pernicious the effects of the humanist-feminist attack on the family has become.

Interviewed by Associated Press writer Linda Deutsch, author Burt Avedon revealed that the psychological effects of the women's movement upon men had inspired his book *Ah, Men!*

"Once proud, bold and secure," he said, men now "seem like the great herds of buffalo that roamed the plains—an endangered species." In gathering material for the book, he interviewed a number of the world's dignitaries and celebrities. He quoted in the AP article what some of them had said. Columnist Art

Buchwald expressed a common feeling when he commented, "Most guys in this country are afraid; somebody else is in charge of their lives." Many of the author's sources see "a coming world of blurred sexual distinctions, an androgynous mix of feminine men and masculine women."

Avedon discerns a significant movement in that direction. "Some of the differences (between the sexes) have already been partially erased," he said, citing the fact that "women are starting to act more like men and men are starting to act a little more sensitive."

He expressed the hope that the sex-role revolution will never be complete, however, asserting that the result would be a world so dull that "there would be little incentive to get up in the morning."

The gravest and most insidious aspect of the attack on the family may be its skill and determination in commandeering the powers of government. In *The Assault on the Sexes*, a book written with her husband, Jim, Andrea Fordham has said:

> *The unisex assault is part of the encompassing trend that seeks to involve the government ever more intimately in our lives through affirmative action programs, quotas, government child-care programs, regulations of the schools, and schemes for sex-role engineering. But the more the government seeks to control the details of our lives, the more the pathology of the ghetto seems to spread into the middle classes, bringing deterioration of family, rising illegitimacy, illiteracy, violent crime, addiction, and venereal disease. The drive to provide equal benefits to groups—neatly legislated and "free" in a gift-wrapped box—*

promises to defeat the kind of liberty that en-
courages the hope, initiative and struggle of
people who prize both civilization and the op-
portunity to shape the destinies of their own
lives.

She warned:

This assault on the traditional dynamic of life
that is sparked between the sexes is being carried
out relentlessly on hundreds of fronts, not merely
through words, slogans, and protests, but by the
diligent acquisition of administrative power
and the methodical changing of regulations and
laws. And I shudder to realize that long before
the last law has been altered, it may already be
too late.

Too late! It may already be too late! We cannot be
sure that it isn't. But I do not believe that it is. If
Christians give themselves to Christ in earnest and
stretch themselves forth in fervent, intercessory prayer,
I believe there is still time to repulse the attack on the
family. If Christians will let Christ live in them and
through them, imbuing them with power and wisdom from on high, I believe there is still time. If
Christians commit themselves to become informed
about the enemy's strategy and ways to combat it,
then become involved in a counterattack to save the
family, I believe there is still time.

Of one thing I am sure, though, and that is that time
is running out. The family is crumbling under the
merciless assault from its enemies.

In the face of such a crisis, it's pointless to speculate
as to whether or not it is too late to act effectively. The
glaring truth is that we must act now because we

cannot act any sooner. It's pointless to debate whether enough time remains for doing all that must be done. We must use whatever time remains because that's all the time we have. The last trumpet call for marriage and the family is being sounded.

Christians and others who adhere to biblical moral principles and God's design for the home must stand strong and united against the attackers. God will not hold us blameless if we sit with hands folded, enjoying our temporary creature comforts, while the forces of darkness destroy the family, our freedom, and our children's future.